CHINA DOCTOR

THE LIFE STORY OF
HARRY WILLIS MILLER

CHINA DOCTOR

THE LIFE STORY OF
HARRY WILLIS MILLER

BY RAYMOND S. MOORE

HARPER & BROTHERS · PUBLISHERS · NEW YORK

To THOSE TEACHERS

WHO HAVE THE VISION TO INSPIRE MEN TO GREATNESS

AND

To THOSE PHYSICIANS

WHOSE FIRST THOUGHT IS TO MAKE MEN WHOLE

CONTENTS

CONTENTS

FOREWORD
by Hollington K. Tong
Ambassador to the United States from the Republic of China, 1956–1958

No book could be more welcome to numerous people the world over than the biography of the great American medical missionary Dr. Harry Willis Miller. Dr. Miller served many peoples in many lands, and my own countrymen, the Chinese, feel particularly fortunate in his long years of service in our country.

I first met Dr. Miller in Shanghai in 1907, only four years after his arrival in China. Already many Chinese had special reason to be grateful to him for his medical services; needy persons who could not afford to enter hospitals received as careful attention from him as did those who could afford to pay.

In addition to my friendship with Dr. Miller, there is a family association that I would like to mention. When Mrs. Bothilde Miller, aunt of the doctor's wife Marie, came to China, it was my wife who taught her the Shanghai dialect.

Coming as Dr. Miller did from a farm family of modest means, he had the initiative and determination to acquire a sound medical education. He became a renowned surgeon, pre-eminent as a thyroid specialist, and made valuable contributions to medical literature.

Dr. Miller is best remembered in China for his treatment of many thousands of patients in sanitariums and clinics established, under his leadership, in Shanghai, Hankow, and other major cities. After the fall of mainland China to the Communists, Dr. Miller took the lead in establishing Taiwan Sanitarium in Taipei, Formosa.

The Chinese people also have reason to be grateful to Dr. Miller for developing and popularizing soy milk as a satisfactory substitute for animal milk, thus helping greatly in the battle against the malnutrition which has always afflicted the people of the Far East. The Chinese have for many ages drunk soy soup for its cooling effect, but they were unaware of the soybean's protein value or that, in the more readily digestible soy-milk form, it could benefit persons suffering from allergies. Since my first acquaintance with Dr. Miller, I have kept myself informed of his activities, especially in the field of nutrition.

Dr. Miller's contribution to the cause of Christianity has been no less important than his contribution in the field of medicine. Through his efforts thousands of persons were converted to the Christian faith in the half century in which he labored in the Far East. Many of them were patients of his, patients inspired by his selfless service to join the faith which made such service possible.

During his long years of religious and medical work in China, Dr. Miller made many friends, a number of whom now hold influential Government positions. The gratitude of both the Government and the people for his work was expressed tangibly when President Chiang Kai-shek decorated him in 1956.

I know that many persons join with me in expressing thanks to Dr. Raymond S. Moore for giving us this opportunity to have a deeper insight into the life and work of a man who is remembered by the people, to whose physical and spiritual needs he so gloriously ministered, as a great American missionary, as a great man.

Taipei, Formosa
January, 1961

PREFACE

It was in 1952 that I first met Harry Miller. Word had arrived at the Japanese college (*Nihon San-iku Gakuin*) of which I was president, that the great China surgeon was coming through again, and that he might visit our school. I knew from experience that meeting legendary figures can be disappointing. But not so with Dr. Miller. During the days he was with us, all were impressed by his simplicity and self-restraint—his sparing meals, early rising, and preference to walk instead of ride.

His curiosity and attention to detail were remarkable, and his willingness to listen gave strength to his quiet counsel. We were honored merely by his presence, but before he left us he volunteered a ten-thousand-dollar gift of equipment for nutritional research. His humble and generous actions and his thoughtfulness will long be remembered.

Here was a brilliant physician who, at twenty-three, had given up a promising instructorship and practice in one of America's medical schools for service under ominous circumstances in a suspicious, even mysterious land. At a time when some missionaries were becoming self-satisfied mercenaries and darkening the colonial cloud, he turned his back on a quarter-million-dollar inheritance to live primitively with the oriental people on

a few cents a day. Thus he demonstrated one of his basic beliefs:
To preach the Christian Way effectively, one must first practice
it in daily life. To our mission group, established in relative
comfort in Japan, his life was a symbol of service beyond our ken.

He ministered to missionaries regardless of denomination, Protestant and Catholic alike. He served his own nation broadly,
including work with the American Relief Administration headed
by Herbert Hoover. Jack of many trades and master of some,
Harry Miller was also consulting physician to two presidents
of the United States—Taft and Wilson. He treated nearly every
important ruler of China from the founding of the Republic,
not to mention unnumbered ambassadors, senators, and princes
of invention and industry around the world. Yet he regarded
these accomplishments simply as doorways to greater service—the
uplift of the underprivileged, the feeding of the famished, and
the tender healing of the unfortunate sick. Because of the generosity of wealthy patients and interested friends, Dr. Miller has
been able to spend fortunes in a lifelong devotion to this cause.

Although he is a distinguished surgeon, the *prevention* of disease has always been his driving goal. He believed that the good
earth of China could provide healthful life for its poor, and that
out of the lessons learned there, the world could help its own.
At first he did not know what this entailed—a cruel alchemist's
mixture of starvation, disease, desperation, and death. But his
certain faith in a personal God lifted him above every obstacle,
and his courage carried him through.

He met almost every challenge in Harry Miller fashion—head
on. But his stubborn, fearlessly resolute and unhesitating character was tempered by an almost infinite patience. Years in the
Orient tend to make one that way. He was no paragon. He did not
pretend to perfection, but when he did make mistakes, they were
in the context of selfless devotion to his fellow men. What to his
colleagues often appeared impulse was more often calculated

action, thought through, quickly or cautiously as the occasion demanded, by a brilliant, keenly disciplined mind.

He was a driving force in the establishment and operation of dozens of hospitals around the world. He has served as consultant for United Nations agencies in attempts to find food for a hungry world. At the age of eighty-one, he has started a new hospital in Hong Kong and has begun to build a foundation for a nutritional program in the Far East which will probably save millions of lives.

His life is a hallmark of service, a tribute to loving parents who could distinguish between fancy and firmness, indulgence and love. It reflects time and again the priceless influence of his dedicated teacher at the Pattytown, Ohio, school, and those other instructors at American Medical Missionary College in Michigan, forerunner of California's College of Medical Evangelists of Loma Linda University—the largest medical school west of the Mississippi—which has supplied a stream of doctors in the Miller tradition to carry American medicine around the world. Speaking of this group of physicians one day while visiting Tokyo Sanitarium and Hospital, United States Ambassador John M. Allison told me, "These men are doing a job for our country that we in the embassies cannot do. I don't know what we could do without them."

The Miller story has been told in parts at palace table and peasant hut, by patients, peons, generals, and kings. Editors, publishers, and broadcasters often urged the doctor to share his experiences. I, too, hoped that he would. One day, to my astonishment, he walked into my Washington, D.C., office and laid his notes on my desk. I knew I could never do justice to the narrative, but there was no turning him down. I have relied heavily on the aid of a number of "old China hands." Especially helpful in providing and checking information were Allan Boynton, Elizabeth Redelstein, E. C. Wood, Raymond F. Cottrell, Adlai Esteb, and the late N. F. Brewer. And of particular help in preparation of the manuscript were Helen Smith, Donna Spotts, and my wife, Dorothy. Invaluable editorial assistance was rendered by Lisa McGaw. Here, for the first time, a few of the details of Harry Miller's distinguished life are pieced together for all to read.

RAYMOND S. MOORE

New York City
January, 1961

CHINA DOCTOR

THE LIFE STORY OF
HARRY WILLIS MILLER

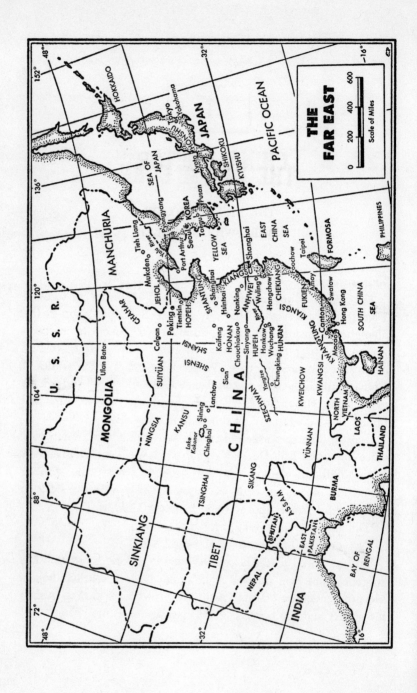

THE OPIUM CURE

"SHOOT HIM!"

The gaunt young commander snapped his order to General T'an, tossing his head in the direction of the south room in the Shanghai mansion, where a middle-aged American surgeon waited. The high-ranking officer expected his orders to be carried out with customary swiftness. Wasn't he marshal of the armies of China, responsible only to the Generalissimo himself? Indeed, he was Chang Hsüeh-liang, ruler of Manchuria, the wealthy and famed "Young Marshal" of the Chinese Republic.

General T'an stepped deliberately into the doctor's temporary office down the hall. He nodded soberly toward the commander's room. Without waiting for the general's words the graying American, elbows on desk, his squared jaws resting solidly in his powerful hands, spoke coolly in fluent Chinese.

"Did he tell you to take my head?"

"Not exactly. But you have the right idea."

"Just as I told you. This means we are making progress." The surgeon's blue eyes warmed as he spoke, his long sensitive fingers accenting a certain oriental quality of his features as they pushed his cheeks and the corners of his eyes upward.

"Except that his own physicians are still giving him the blossom of the poppy." The general was dubious.

The situation was more than serious. At that moment in a very real and singular sense, missionary Harry Willis Miller, M.D., F.A.C.S., was responsible for the future of China. As a well man, the Young Marshal had been a beloved genius. Now desperately sick and wasted from opium addiction, he was a hazard and a handicap to the Central Government. Many would welcome his death. However, if he were to die, it might trigger a national uprising. Because of his losses in the north he was in bad repute with the military and must take temporary leave from China. Yet no foreign state would accept him in his condition.

The Young Marshal was a brilliant field commander, but in devilish fashion opium had purchased his body and was negotiating for his soul. His Manchurian armies were bowing to Japan's invaders, not so much from superior force and tactics as from his personal dereliction. The drug-racked commander had already been pushed or scared from Mukden down to Peking, his courage burned out by the opium pipe.

Basically a kind and unusually gentle man, the Young Marshal was driven to dope by the constant conflict between his own personality and the ruthless demands of his military assignment. The eldest son of a powerful Manchurian ruler, "Old Marshal" Chang Tso-lin, the Young Marshal was noted for his wealth as well as for his military acumen. He would shrewdly convert his paper money into silver and deposit it outside of Manchuria in such banks as New York's National City or Chase National.

It was well known that the Japanese had long plotted the downfall of Chang Tso-lin, and they were commonly blamed for his death by a bomb explosion on June 4, 1928. Expecting a collapse of the Manchurian Government at the death of the old strong man, they promptly made overwhelming demands on his mild-mannered son. However, the clever Young Marshal managed to keep secret for a week the fact of his father's death, which gave him needed time to reorganize the Government.

Although he ran a tight military dictatorship in Manchuria, the young commander had an abiding concern for his people and their welfare. From Madame Chiang Kai-shek he had heard much about Shanghai Sanitarium, opened in 1928 by the Seventh-day Adventist Church, largely through Dr. Miller's efforts. He longed for a similar institution at Mukden, his capital. From the wealthy Young Marshal's point of view, financing such an institution was not the principal problem. Rather was it a question of staffing a hospital and procuring equipment.

In the meanwhile, persons in Shanghai were urging the establishment of a hospital in Manchuria. To them, the lack of money was a major obstacle. And so it happened that in 1932 when the Young Marshal was himself anxious to establish a Mukden Sanitarium, two women—Dr. Miller's wife, Marie, and her friend, Mrs. John Oss—arrived in Mukden to solicit funds for a Manchurian hospital. They carried with them a letter Dr. Miller had obtained from the Young Marshal's close friend, General Chang Chüin, then mayor of Shanghai and later secretary general to Chiang Kai-shek on Formosa.

Normally, officials had to wait for days for an audience with Marshal Chang, but when he learned that two women wished to talk with him about establishing a hospital, he called them in without delay.

Startled at finding the Young Marshal so emaciated and pale, the women were reluctant to ask him for anything. But when with a friendly smile he asked, "What can I do for you?" they took courage.

"The China Division of the Church—the Seventh-day Adventist Church—would like to start some medical work in northern Manchuria," they told him. "We have been thinking about building a hospital one hundred fifty miles or so north of Mukden where Dr. Martin Vinkel already has set up a temporary clinic, and we were wondering if you would give us the names of individuals who might be interested in such a venture."

"How much money do you need?" he asked them, his evident interest only partially concealing his weariness.

"We were hoping possibly for thirty thousand dollars," they said cautiously.

"You will need a whole lot more than that to start a medical institution for Manchuria," he replied firmly. "This is a big place. Never mind about soliciting anybody else. I will give you one hundred thousand dollars to start."

The women did not know what to do. They had never dreamed of anything like this. They replied weakly that it was wonderful, but they would have to go back and talk with their leaders at Shanghai.

"Who is this you have to confer with?" he asked them.

"Mrs. Miller's husband—and other persons with the China Division," Mrs. Oss replied.

"You bring Dr. Miller here." The Young Marshal's overtones suggested a command.

A few days later Dr. Miller arrived in Mukden. As Miller recalls it: "The Young Marshal made these propositions: He wanted a hospital in Mukden. It must be the best, and he not only would give us one hundred thousand dollars, but would provide us all the land we wanted in Mukden's beautiful memorial park, the finest area in the city.

"Obviously it was a Providential opening, for up until then no building had been permitted in the beautifully wooded park, and now our group was invited to stake off all the land we wanted. Before long, we had a fine walled compound with a sanitarium and hospital, and homes for doctors and nurses, all a personal gift from the Young Marshal."*

Against this background W. H. Donald, the Young Marshal's astute adviser from Australia, had approached Harry Miller one day in 1933. Wise in matters of the Far East, he, along with James Elder, a thoroughly trustworthy financial man, was largely responsible for the business affairs of the Young Marshal. He and Elder had come to Miller's office at Shanghai Sanitarium, and were seated before the surgeon.

"Dr. Miller," Donald began, his voice and expression betraying a profound gravity, "the time has come when we have to do something about the Marshal's addiction. The Generalissimo and T. V. Soong agree, and the Marshal himself is anxious for a cure." T. V. Soong was treasurer of the Chinese Government and a close friend of the Young Marshal. Miller knew that Marshal Chang had tried the opium cure in Mukden several years before, without success, and later at the Rockefeller Medical Center in Peking with the same discouraging results.

The Young Marshal's condition was now more grave than ever—so serious, in fact, that during official conferences or interviews, his doctors had to come in every fifteen or twenty minutes to give him an injection, usually of strong and powerful drugs. He was entirely dependent upon them for sleep or bodily rest of any kind. Still worse, his two wives had become addicted, also.

"We have heard of your success with opium cures and wonder if you would come to see what you can do for the Young Marshal," Donald said. "The national situation is so complex that if something is not done soon the Generalissimo fears the danger of a major rebellion, and we can't afford this now, with the Japanese pressing in from the north and the Communists from the west."

* This was in 1933, after the Japanese had established the puppet state Manchukuo.

Dr. Miller was well aware of the political crisis. Frequently, members of the Generalissimo's cabinet, sometimes Chiang Kai-shek himself, met at the Sanitarium, carefully stationing guards at the outer gates, throughout the compound, and at their doors.

"I have work here which I cannot leave," the doctor demurred. "I will undertake the cure on three conditions: First, the Young Marshal and his family must be brought to Shanghai." This was quite an undertaking because he was always accompanied by a large bodyguard of both Russians and Chinese, so mixed in order to avoid any plots that might be hatched by a clique if the guards were of one nationality only.

"Second," Dr. Miller specified, "his two wives must take the cure with him." He was not underestimating the influence of women.

"And third, General T'an, his chief of staff, must understand that I have absolute authority over the Marshal and his bodyguard until the cure is completed."

General T'an's dependability was above question. He had been one of Miller's patients, and felt that he owed his life to the American doctor. There is no one more loyal than a devoted Chinese.

It was impossible to arrange accommodations for the Young Marshal and his large staff at the Sanitarium, so it was agreed to undertake treatment at his Shanghai mansion nearby. On the appointed day Dr. Miller took some nurses and went to the mansion. After lingering longer than the busy surgeon was accustomed to, he saw one of the Young Marshal's doctors coming down to the general waiting room.

"Could I do something for you?" the doctor asked Miller somewhat superciliously.

"I am here at the request of the Marshal," the American replied. "We are undertaking his cure from the drug."

"Just how do you plan to treat him?" the Chinese physician asked.

"We have our own plan," Harry Miller told him with calculated restraint. "I don't think it will be necessary to go over the details. It is the Marshal we are treating." It would have been disastrous to describe his treatment to the Chinese doctor, for he was one of those profiteering from the drugs administered to the beleaguered Marshal.

Furthermore, the projected therapy easily could have precipitated harmful professional comment. It was the doctor's intention to use cantharides, a drug commonly known as "Spanish fly," which actually had little direct relationship to the cure itself. He used it on addicts more as a distraction than as a direct therapy. The cantharides developed a blister when applied to the skin area. He then injected a serum from the blister, under aseptic conditions, and the psychological effect was salutary, in fact almost amazing.

Because of the weakened moral fiber of victims, many opium "cures" are not permanent, but the Young Marshal was a man of unusual stamina and determination. His prognosis would be excellent if the proper conditions were met.

"Well, whom do you want to treat first?" the Chinese doctor next inquired of Miller.

"We will start with the Marshal," Miller replied, "and after we have him well under way we will treat his wives."

"But we think you should start on the wives first, and if they get along all right then try the Marshal." The Chinese was now speaking for his fellow physicians who were contriving against the cure. By this time Dr. Miller was becoming impatient.

"We will begin with the Marshal as I have said," he answered firmly, then turned and left.

In a matter of hours the Young Marshal called Miller back to the mansion, where he was met by the same doctor with the

same rigmarole. Once more Miller returned to the Sanitarium,
certain that the Young Marshal and General T'an would seek him
out. They did. This time Donald was sent down to see Miller
and inquire why the treatment was not begun.

"When you get those doctors out of my way so that I can
get past the entry hall we will start," the American replied, re-
lating the happenings of the past few hours.

There were no further delays; but when Dr. Miller was ushered
in to see the Young Marshal, his heart fell at the prospect of
the miserable addict. Could he ever respond? Madame Chang,
the first wife of the Young Marshal, was also frail, now weighing
only eighty-four pounds. The second wife, Miss Elsie Chow, appeared younger and stronger.*

"Well," the Young Marshal began after the greetings, "here I
am. I will do whatever you want me to do."

"Now, Marshal," Miller told him guardedly, "I have taken
others through this cure and I am going to be very careful with
you. I will do the best I know how, and will stay right with you
and look after you myself. There is no reason why we cannot
succeed. But it must be very clearly understood that I have
complete authority over this place, including your bodyguard,
your staff, and your physicians. You must understand that they
are to take orders from no one but me; not from you or anyone
else. There must be no reservations. No matter what you say
under any and all circumstances, I am to have complete authority. If you agree to that we will succeed. If you don't, there
is no point in going ahead." Dr. Miller was well aware, from
many previous experiences, of the agonies and commotions at-
tending these cures, and of the intensified temptation.

Without hesitation the Young Marshal called his chief of staff.

"General T'an," he instructed, "you're to listen only to Dr.

* Technically, Madame Chang was the Young Marshal's only wife. Elsie
Chow, also a cultured and highly educated woman, was generally known as
his "second wife" but was called "Miss Chow."

Miller. He has complete control and authority over this household and will be given anything he wants. Listen to him and only him, follow his instructions and orders explicitly, I command you." The Young Marshal and Miller knew that faithful General T'an would carry out those commands implicitly and rigorously.

Turning to the American, the Young Marshal said, "I put myself wholly in your hands." Satisfied, Dr. Miller started the treatments—first an enema and then a rectal anesthetic which placed the Young Marshal in a sound sleep. At this point the Sanitarium team arranged things in the house for more efficient operation. The Young Marshal's bed was replaced with a hospital bed. They found tablets which the physicians had stuffed under the sheets, pillows, and even in the mattress itself. This was not unexpected.

A few hours later, after the Marshal had been started on his program, Madame Chang called to ask why she was not being treated.

"Pretty soon he'll be well and I'll be left in addiction," she said fearfully.

"We thought it wise to take the Marshal first, to see how things go," Miller spoke to her reassuringly. Actually, he wanted to be certain that the Young Marshal was progressing favorably before undertaking her case, which involved more risk because of her extremely poor physical condition.

"But I want you to start now—today," she insisted. Her earnestness finally persuaded Miller to go ahead. Miss Chow, on the other hand, was not so eager for the cure. But she realized she could not be addicted while the other two were cured, so she braced up and began, although at the time her co-operation was less noteworthy than that of the others.

Intravenous medications kept up their body fluids, and less habit-forming sedatives were substituted for the opium. By the third day the nurses, under Dr. Miller's close supervision, began easing up on sedation, quite aware of the probability of diarrhea, vomiting, severe cramps and muscle aches, a condition which could last for several days. Hot compresses and other physical remedies minimized these withdrawal symptoms and kept the patients as comfortable as possible. Later all sedatives were discontinued, causing even greater pain and discomfort for the patients.

Madame Chang held up remarkably well and went through the entire routine with great courage. Miss Chow showed less fortitude; but the Marshal was the noisy one. Finally he refused to take anything by mouth and had to be fed by tube. He began to complain loudly that the Americans were abusing him. He could be heard over the entire mansion.

It was about this time that Miller began to realize the Chinese doctors were seeking to set the guards against the Sanitarium team, hoping in that way to sabotage the cure.

Dr. Miller turned abruptly to General T'an, hands now firmly on the edge of the desk. The picture was quite clear. The Young Marshal's three Chinese doctors were determined to block his opium cure. His addiction had made them handsome profits. The American doctor and his treatments must go—even if he had to be shot.

"Get that quack and his opium ring out of this house! I don't care how, but get them out!" Miller commanded in a low voice level with authority though threaded with concern.

Later in the day the general returned to the missionary's office. "They are gone," he reported simply.

Surprised and gratified at this speed, the doctor expressed curiosity about his method.

"Very simple," General T'an assured him with oriental modesty. "I went to them and said, 'You hear the Marshal making a lot of racket. He is now quite determined that someone will give him the drug, and that would undo the whole affair. But if somebody does give him something—though I know you men wouldn't do it—naturally the American doctor is going to suspect that since you men possess the medicine, you are the ones to blame. Now I have been ordered by T. V. Soong, treasurer of the Government, that if anybody interferes with Dr. Miller or slips some medicine to the Marshal he shall be summarily shot. While I know you men wouldn't do it and I should hate to shoot you, that might be demanded by the Government if the doctor suspects you are the ones that interfered. He has complete authority and I am bound to carry out his orders. Could it be that you prefer not to linger here?' Well, those men couldn't get their clothes together quickly enough. They made a dive for the railway station and jumped the train for North China. *Che wei jen yu pan shih i-yang ying*—They now believe that the American is a very hard rock."

After General T'an sent the doctors on their way in panic for northern China, Miller turned to deal with the Young Marshal. The crisis had arrived. Going through the tortures of the damned, he became violent. The doctor, determined not to give him the comfort of sedation and thus prolong his cure, wrestled physically with him until finally the Young Marshal began to wilt completely. Then he started to cry.

It was a strangely unreal experience for the missionary doctor, sitting there on that warm June day in 1933 with one of the great field commanders of the Orient, the ruler of Manchuria, sobbing like a child. And then the Young Marshal told him a story which had been locked closely in his heart.

"My father was a military man, and required that I, the eldest son, should follow in his steps," he confided. "I never wanted to be a general. I simply wanted a professional education. But I was forced to go along with the Chinese tradition which requires the eldest son to follow in the footsteps of his father and to be the family head. When I would go out to battle and my soldiers killed a lot of people, it caused me such pain and anxiety that I didn't know what to do. I felt so sorry for those poor people who were being shot, because I knew that they were not guilty of any crime, and had as much right as I to live.

"And then on some occasions it became my terrifying duty to have to condemn some men to death. This all haunted me so much that the only way I could get any rest was to smoke the poppy. And soon after I started my wife fell into the practice with me, and opium took over our home like a horrible disease. Miss Chow also became addicted. I am eternally grateful to you for this cure."

A few days later arrangements were completed for one of Miller's colleagues, Dr. Read Calvert, a Shanghai Sanitarium nurse, and W. H. Donald to accompany Marshal Chang and his family to Europe. This was considered wise, not only for his own recuperation, but because of still-smoldering reactions from his military failures in the north. Before leaving to board the ship, however, the Young Marshal demonstrated his gratitude in an unusual way. Calling Dr. Miller to his room, he sat the doctor down beside the bed.

"Dr. Miller, I have settled all my bills for the care here, and have paid for all the help from the Sanitarium. Now I want to do something for you personally." Then, in the presence of Dr. Calvert, he handed Harry Miller an envelope. "Get yourself an airplane or a house," he instructed. "Remember, whatever you do, this is for you alone."

Dr. Miller expressed his appreciation, and after the manner of the Orient placed the envelope in his pocket, to be opened later when he was out of the presence of his benefactor. "I had an optimistic idea," Miller says, "that it was probably a check for anywhere from five hundred dollars to five thousand dollars, which of course would be an unusually fine personal gift. But when I went outside and opened the envelope I found a bank draft for fifty thousand dollars made out to me! For once I was dumfounded.

"But I knew it would not be right for me to accept money.

By now we had two hundred workers in the China field and each was doing his part just as faithfully as I was. Besides, I thought of the nurses and doctors at the Sanitarium who were working day and night to keep up their end of things. After a little conference, Marie and I decided to put the money in the bank for a badly needed hospital at Lanchow in the great northwest territory of China. This meant the Young Marshal had not only given us Mukden Sanitarium, but now one at Lanchow as well."

Some time later W. H. Donald recounted the events of the Young Marshal's European trip. He told Dr. Miller how he had observed the new spring in Marshal Chang's step. "Marshal, you are a different man," he had told him enthusiastically. "You have a lot to be thankful for to have a man like Dr. Miller cure you."

The young commander, turning to Donald, had replied with deep conviction, "Yes, I am thankful to Dr. Miller. But you know, it was God who healed me."

For the dedicated missionary doctor the knowledge that his patient had given the credit to God brought a thrill he never forgot.

Later, Donald again appeared at Harry Miller's Shanghai office.

"The Marshal sent me down to see you, Dr. Miller. And do you know what he wants you to do?"

"No, I haven't the slightest idea," he replied. "How is the Marshal?"

"The Marshal is well, very well, and is determined to have a sanitarium in Hankow just like the one you have here in Shanghai."

Miller was well aware of the needs of Hankow, known as the Chicago of the Orient.

"I'm not sure just what to say," he replied. "At the present time we are building a hospital in Canton, another at Calgan, and are just getting under way in the hospital we built in Manchuria. Building a hospital is one thing, but staffing and equipping it are quite another. It takes money to run them."

"Money isn't a problem at all," Donald assured him. "The only question is whether you will undertake to find the personnel and to run the institution. The Marshal will give you the land and the funds for the building, and will personally subsidize its operation."

A few weeks later after careful investigation by Pastor M. E. Warren of the Hankow district, E. C. Wood, architect and builder, and others of the Church leaders, a cablegram was sent to the Washington headquarters of the Seventh-day Adventist Church requesting permission to accept the Young Marshal's offer. "And a few months later we were building Wuhan Sanitarium on a beautiful tract of land on Hankow's East Lake at Wuchang, south of the Yangtze River," says Dr. Miller. "Furthermore, Generalissimo Chiang Kai-shek, a great believer in our medical work, was in it with the Marshal, adding one hundred thousand dollars to the fund. Still later Madame Chiang Kai-shek spent twenty thousand dollars for a residence on the grounds so she could come for treatments whenever she was in the area."

To Harry Miller and his helpers it continued to be a wonder that an overruling Providence had used an opium-ridden army general to provide hospitals for ten thousand sick around Hankow and Lanchow, and had picked a rock-hard American from a midwest farm to push aside some unscrupulous Chinese doctors and to cure their victim.

II

HALLWAY TO SERVICE

FROM OHIO FARM BOY to China Doctor was, for Harry Miller, the simple and logical fulfillment of a dedicated life. Naïve, rugged, and mischievous, he had lived a Tom Sawyer boyhood. Brilliant, stubborn, and courageous, he had walked frontier paths, his maturing ambitions leading him on—like a fledgling but persistent mountaineer who looks hopefully at each rise as the peak, only to find that it is but another step in a much longer trek to the top.

The first of five children of Amanda Ehlers and John Oliver Miller, Harry was born at Ludlow Falls, Ohio, on July 1, 1879, in a small log cabin near Grandfather Ehlers' stone quarry.

The Millers and the Ehlerses all knew the dignity of manual labor, which Harry was to learn also. Ironically, however, because of an early misfortune, John Miller had become the educated member of the family. He lost his left thumb and forefinger in a cane-mill accident. Concerned that his handicap might disqualify him for skilled trades, his parents had provided him an education to be a teacher. John Miller fostered in his son the goal of higher education.

At the elementary school in Pattytown, where the Millers had moved from adjacent Ludlow Falls, a wise schoolmaster further pointed the way. With evangelistic zeal he held the torch of service and leadership before his students. Harry caught his vision. At Ohio's Mount Vernon Academy, a puritan-strict boarding school, those dreams began to crystallize into action. The academy's balanced program of work, study, and worship buttressed the boy's natural qualities of frugality, dependability, and sobriety.

As his senior year wore on, Harry became deeply troubled. Some of his classmates were talking about teaching, others about the ministry, and still others about business. He was not ungrateful for his education, and he knew he wanted more, but for what he was not sure until an unexpected circumstance turned his thoughts toward medicine.

Word came of the opening of a new medical school—American Medical Missionary College—in Battle Creek, Michigan, where the young Seventh-day Adventist Church, to which the Millers belonged, had opened its first medical establishment in 1866. As the largest medical institution in America in the 1890's Battle Creek Sanitarium, with facilities to care for fourteen hundred patients, was giving the little Michigan town a world reputation as a health center. Under the leadership of Dr. John Harvey Kellogg, it had become well known for its physical therapy and treatment of chronic diseases. Sometimes as many as three thousand persons would be registered there at one time, the sixteen hundred overflow patients being housed in surrounding hotels, apartments, homes, and even in private railroad cars. It also became the birthplace of modern dietetics. There Dr. Kellogg and his brother Will Keith (W. K.) began their experiments in nutrition which eventually developed into the modern American breakfast-food industry.

It was at a camp meeting the summer following his graduation from the academy that Harry's curiosity flared into conviction when Dr. Daniel H. Kress of the faculty of American Medical Missionary College advised the Ohio boy to study medicine, and arranged for his matriculation at that school in the fall of 1898. His was the fourth class in the college.

The decision to study medicine meant surmounting serious obstacles. The most overwhelming for the ambitious young student was his terror of blood or of death. As a child he had listened to his uncles tell ghost stories around the fireside. Their tales of the strange and terrifying things that happened at night made a strong impression on his young mind and produced a desperate and ungodly fear of the dark, of graveyards, and of the dead. When one of the students at the academy died of pneumonia, Harry stayed in his room to avoid seeing even the coffin or the hearse. He wondered how he would ever manage to be a physician.

There was another hurdle to leap. He was barely nineteen, and without a penny. At camp meeting he had been encouraged to sell religious books as a means of earning money. He viewed the idea dimly; yet there was little choice, so he started out through the countryside that summer with his prospectus, eating at a different table and sleeping in a different house—or barn— every night. He learned to know the snug friendliness of the fence rows where he could take an occasional nap without notice of passers-by.

Frugality and perseverance brought Harry the necessary sum for school entrance. But the greatest profit from his summer's travels was not material. "I learned more about meeting and dealing with people than ever before," he recalls. "I had learned before to know animals well, but I knew little about people. I came to enjoy watching their eyes and answering their questions as I recited my canvass. There stirred in my heart an obligation for service which I am sure led me to medical ministry."

Harry's emotions oscillated between anticipation and foreboding as he arrived at Battle Creek for the fall term. The president made it clear from the start that the new class would have

two sets of teachers—the regular faculty and the sophomores.
Part of the instruction would be at Battle Creek and the remainder at Chicago in connection with Cook County Hospital.

Even in those days a student enjoyed a singular sense of status
when accepted into a medical college. Each freshman vied with
his classmates in telling of his remarkable career before entering
medical school and in emphasizing the tremendous amount of
learning he possessed. Each made it clear that he had graduated
from the most important school, and underscored his opinion that
there was very little more for him to learn.

Harry soon discovered that he had overlooked one piece of
instruction contained in the religious books he had sold: "Pride
goeth before a fall." Anatomy was a catastrophe, dry as its own
bones, a motley and meaningless conglomeration of tissues and
organs. His pride in being the youngest member of the class
shifted to deep concern. He never forgot his first recitation.

"What is the epiphysis of this bone?" The professor nodded
in Harry's direction. Harry remembered that it had been in the
lesson, but that was all he remembered.

"I don't believe I can answer that question," he replied, borrow-
ing on his old boldness.

"What then is the diaphysis?"

Again, Harry remembered that it had been in the lesson, but
it had failed to click. He knew that one was the round end of
the bone and the other was its shaft. But which was which? He
stood there, handkerchief at his forehead, suddenly as wilted as
week-old graveside flowers, and just about as sad.

"That will do, Miller," the professor said.

Harry sat down, excruciatingly embarrassed, defeated in his
first recitation in medical school. "It was probably the best thing
that ever happened to me," he now believes. "I determined that
I would read over and over and memorize every chapter, if
necessary. I would never have that humiliating experience again.

It soon became obvious to us all that those professors knew exactly how to take the starch out of freshmen."

His friend Stoops from Oklahoma was the bright boy of the class. The professor called his name one day.

"Name the structures that pass under the inguinal ligament," he said. Stoops named them glibly, but one that he named belonged to a different group. The teacher did not correct him. He simply said:

"That will do, Stoops."

The next day the professor called on Stoops again, firing the same question. Stoops confidently repeated the same answer.

"That will do, Stoops." The instructor did not correct him.

The third time the professor called on Stoops the whole class began to snicker and laugh. That time the boy sat down confused and worried. The professor did not have to ask a fourth time.

Harry Miller's summer profits did not last long. He joined the ranks of other freshmen who met expenses by beating carpets for the matron, or by repairing equipment, or by nursing at the Sanitarium. At Battle Creek Sanitarium, diet was king, and it ruled well. That was why people went there. In all of the treatment was the constant admonition that the well-being of the body derived directly from diet. Those lessons were more important to Harry than he knew, and they were to bear fruit around the world in later years. Nursing in the wing that housed mental patients was the work which Harry found most difficult. He would take his books, hoping to have a chance to study, but there would be little chance for book learning with patients walking around the room mumbling and making threats, or pacing near one of the windows high above the sidewalk.

Psychotic patients in the Sanitarium were not the only problem persons. Harry soon realized that many on the outside were worse off than those within. He was given a job in the hospital's maintenance department to help repair batteries, which were used in those days to stir up the patients' nerves and improve their muscles by vibrating their hands and arms. He considered himself lucky to get that kind of job, until he discovered the man in charge cared for no one, and no one cared for him.

"Go over and fix that battery," the electrician would command without a word of instruction about how to do it. No sooner had the young assistant dissected it than the electrician would come around and ask, "What in the world are you doing?" Whereupon, he would deliver a lengthy rebuke while demonstrating the repair technique he should have outlined in the first place.

Not all of medical school's lessons derived from Gray's *Anatomy* and histology lab, Harry was learning. Indeed, medicine seemed more and more to be a matter of learning how to deal with the human mind.

III

THE MEDICAL BUFF

BATTLE CREEK was the highest point in the state of Michigan, and the Weather Bureau set up an observation post in the Sanitarium tower. Taking the instrument readings three times a day was a coveted job, especially for the freshmen, who usually got the crumbs. Harry heard of a vacancy and became a cloud watcher. His duties were to record the readings from the barometer, the wet-bulb thermometer and the dry-weather thermometer, to check the velocity of the wind on the aerometer, and to check and report the direction of the wind and the condition and types of the clouds. That took about fifteen minutes, and the Weather Bureau gave an hour's credit for it.

Harry soon learned that every job has its disciplines. Keeping the appointments three times a day at exactly the hour required was more of a strain than he had anticipated. A few weeks of that was enough. He arranged for his roommate, Stoops, to take the job. Stoops proceeded to demonstrate how it should be done.

"This idea of going up to the top of the Sanitarium morning, noon, and night is no fun," Stoops complained, as if Harry did not already know it. "I'm going to bring the instruments down here to my room, hang the barometer outside, and poke the aerometer through the open window. I can see all the clouds from here, anyway."

Several weeks later when he sent in his monthly record it was so far out of line that the Weather Bureau investigated, and for the second time Stoops learned the penalty of intelligence without wisdom: He was fired.

As a direct result of that momentary foolishness Stoops did his roommate one of the best turns of his life when he finagled a job helping with post-mortems and picking up after them. Stoops would come home with elaborate accounts of how he sewed them up, and what he did with them. He was well aware that these reports were received with loathing. Struggling to conceal his old fear of a corpse, Harry was glad Stoops did not know that he used to run into a cornfield to hide from passing funerals, but he feared that some day Stoops would discover the abysmal depths of his cowardice.

"Come down and help me," Stoops would urge with fiendish pleasure at his friend's discomfort.

"I have studying to do," Harry would protest weakly.

"But where can you learn more about the human body than dealing with it firsthand?" Stoops would tighten the winch on him.

"I will study corpses when I take pathology," Harry would reply, with scant comfort from his conscience.

Finally, one night Stoops lowered the boom.

"There is an old lady that died in a fall down the San steps," he reported, "and we are going to have a post-mortem in the basement of James White Memorial. Come on over." Harry made up another feeble excuse, and then the boom hit him where it hurt worst.

"I bet you're a coward; you're afraid to go," Stoops jeered.

The blow could not have been more precisely aimed. If word got around that he was timid, his fellow students would dog the life out of him—maybe put a kidney in his pocket, part of a dead person in his bed, anything to throw him into hysterics from fear. He could not risk that reputation at any cost.

"Of course I'll go," Harry answered, with perhaps the boldest hypocrisy and most studied nonchalance a man ever mustered. He went, scared and trembling all the way. To make matters worse, post-mortems were held at night. He prayed; but he had learned that God helps those who help themselves. Perhaps he could peek in the door, just a glimpse to see if he could take it. But what if he fainted?

Suddenly the door opened and there they were, a whole room full of fellows with the corpse in the middle. Immediately, inexplicably, the whole sense of nervousness and fear dissolved.

From that moment Harry Miller became so interested in anatomy and so thoroughly its master that long before his graduation he was marked for a professorship. After that crisis night, he applied for work in the laboratory. It was his job to put on an old raincoat, load the vaseline-covered cadavers over his shoulder, and carry them up from the cellar to the spring-wagon which would transport them to the laboratory a block away. He reflected on the Harry he used to be as he watched the Negro boy who drove the old wagon down to get the corpses, sitting up front, staring fixedly ahead, horrified at the thought of seeing those dead bodies, but knowing that his job depended on hauling them. But for Stoops, Harry thought, I might still be like that boy.

The new Harry, poised, confident, and steel nerved, prefigured the Miller of China, who countless times would coolly face death by bandits, disease, violence, or war, and walk confidently in its shadows.

Few laymen know the cost of medical training. It is more than monetary. There are the thousand adjustments, points of view, dedication to service, and sobering ethical codes that must be graven upon the student's heart. Uncertainty nags at every level: the daily quiz, semester finals, clinical tests, and medical boards.

Merciless are the odd schedules, sleepless nights, and temptations which linger on every hand. Harry Miller found in medical school that when his stomach was empty those problems assumed the specter of doom. Sometimes his hunger was so real that he questioned the high cost of medicine.

His reaction to the emergency was routine: for two pennies he could buy a little sack of Granola, a healthful dry cereal much like finely ground whole-wheat crackers; skim milk was free for the turning on of the faucet. He boiled the milk, poured it over the Granola, and filled up his stomach.

But he paid the inevitable price of lowered resistance from his unbalanced diet, and came down with typhoid fever just as his class was to go to Chicago for six weeks of study in anatomy. Following days of delirium and unconsciousness from the high fever, he made a new resolution: Balanced living is the best economy. And so that summer he sold books again. The newly confident Harry and his medical-school friends, Arthur Selmon and Franklin Richards, proved apt salesmen of John Harvey Kellogg's "men only" and "women only" books: *Man the Masterpiece* and *Ladies' Guide*.

Returning for his sophomore year Harry quickly made up his six weeks' work in anatomy, and happily passed with his class. He took considerable delight in his new job as guide through the Sanitarium and food factory. He lectured enthusiastically on gymnastics, muscle building, vegetarianism, hydrotherapy, and the evils of coffee, tobacco, and narcotics. The food factory was a particularly important place on the guided tour, for samples were served to guests. Since food was one of his main expenses, Harry served himself liberally along with the others.

This experience, too, was to play its role in Harry Miller's future. The processing of foods at Battle Creek aroused his curiosity. He had helped his mother at home and later had served as assistant cook at Mount Vernon Academy, but he had never taken time to find out *why* foods were prepared the way they were.

His ignorance had been clearly exposed the day the academy matron sent him to the springhouse to get a jar of yeast. She told him to smell it to be sure it was all right. That instruction proved a mistake. Not being acquainted with the odor of yeast, he thought it was spoiled and threw it away. The next time she sent him she specified that this time *she* would test it. But on the way back Harry took off the lid, smelled the yeast, and reported that it, too, was spoiled, just as the other had been. The matron was indignant. "To think of all the bread that yeast could have raised," she mourned.

Every such experience provided a certain leaven in Harry's life, and that was well, for big things were just ahead. In his junior and senior years he sat under some of medicine's greatest men: Nicholas Senn, John B. Murphy, and William Osler. From Johns Hopkins University in Baltimore and McGill University in Canada, from Britain and the Continent these and other great lecturers came to Battle Creek and to Rush Medical College, where Harry was also taking courses, to sharpen his wits and deepen his skills.

Harry's senior year brought other adventures, too: his assignment as student teacher in anatomy; the clinical experiences at Chicago and Battle Creek; the new sense of professional responsibility that comes to a medico who realizes that the big day is at hand when he will be on his own. And then there was his classmate, Maude Thompson, who, in those days of new dreams, began to appear more as an attractive woman and less as a classroom competitor.

Courtship in medical school is at best a dubious enterprise, and for a while it had Harry at his wit's end. There was the abiding danger that if a fellow did not spend full time on his books he would fail his course. On the other hand, if he did not give reasonable attention to his girl, he might lose her. There was reason to fear that in the mixed-up process he might lose both. A peculiar new shyness and uncertainty clouded the Miller horizon. He had never gone out with girls before.

He began to take a patronizing interest in Maude "to make sure that she passed the medical course." She did, and so did Harry. They were graduated from American Medical Missionary College in the class of 1902, and were married soon after graduation. However, Harry was caught off base a few days following their marriage when they sat for their state medical examinations in Chicago.

Miller tells the story: "My roommate, Arthur Selmon, and I had been constantly competing, nip and tuck, for top grades in our class. Whether in the lectures at Battle Creek or in the clinics in Chicago, we ran neck and neck. This race, and my assignment as instructor in anatomy, had inflated an already healthy ego. Maude was a serious student, but I made it my business to caution her repeatedly to be thorough in her preparation for the examination. I didn't worry for a moment about my passing.

"Then about a month after the examination the news came. I managed to get by, but alas, Maude's average was two per cent higher than mine. Only two per cent, but I had to live with that a long time."

From his teaching job the young doctor was able to repay a seventy-five-dollar loan from his Aunt Catherine Honeyman, and still have a little cash left for his wedding day. Teaching was interesting but it was not the kind of teaching he had envisioned in Pattytown. He was discovering that first-class teaching is more than giving orders to students, that it is, indeed, leadership of the highest order.

Harry spent long nights preparing his lectures and drawing anatomy "maps" to make the lectures crystal clear. During their internship year at the Chicago clinic—Harry was resident physician there—Maude joined in making them a teaching team, she in obstetrics and gynecology and he in anatomy. At the same time, Harry was making frequent calls to Battle Creek Sanitarium.

In the Chicago clinic, Miller worked under two men, Dr. David

Paulsen, an eminent neurologist, and Dr. W. B. Holden, an unusually able surgeon. With his early fears of the dead, it had once seemed unlikely that Harry would ever be a surgeon, but his experiences with Stoops at Battle Creek apparently made the difference, and Dr. Paulsen unconsciously crystallized his goal.

Dr. Miller describes his teacher as "a great man, widely known through Chicago, and particularly devoted to uplift work with the drug addicts and alcoholics of that city. His 'Life-boat Mission' was the center of his life. It was all he could think of or talk about. He taught us how to sober up his drunks, holding them firmly in the shower and dousing them vigorously with alternate hot and cold water. Sometimes they would rebel and it would take two or three of us to hold them in.

"Dr. Paulsen set us an example of infinite patience and sympathy. After all of his work on those poor fellows, they would be right back a day or two later for the same old treatment over again. Yet he never hesitated to help them. The misery we found in visiting their families almost tore the hearts out of us.

"The opium addicts were even more hopeless than the drunks. In their frenzy they sometimes exhibited unbelievable cleverness in finding more of the miserable drug. Often they would resort to fits or to swinging their chairs to fight their way out of the hospital. One time a patient waited until I turned my head momentarily, grabbed a water pitcher, and broke it in pieces over my head.

"The delirium tremens ward was equally interesting, especially at night. There the terror-stricken patients constantly visioned lions, snakes, and miry creatures crawling all over them. They would fight and flail their imaginary attackers, screaming in horror.

"These experiences and Dr. Paulsen's incessant lecturing on the objectives of the 'Life-boat Mission' contrasted so vividly with a peaceful and systematic program in surgery, that I found myself turning to Dr. Holden's service for sheer release. Before long he gave me the surgical residency in eye, ear, nose, and throat. But since Dr. Paulsen was the anesthetist for my surgical cases, the 'Life-boat Mission' was ever with me.

"Oftentimes while operating I lectured to the medical students. But Dr. Paulsen always managed to get a word in about the 'Life-boat Mission,' and the first thing I knew he would be entertaining them with stories about his 'patients' there. This aggravated me no end, but there was little that I, a young surgeon, could do. Dr. Paulsen was not only a great and wonderful man to whom the students looked with admiration, but he was also medical director of the hospital. Usually I ended up doing my explaining afterwards at the regular recitation period.

"Dr. Paulsen's wife, Mary Wild-Paulsen, was also a physician, a teacher of obstetrics. Maude profited greatly by her association with Dr. Mary. The Paulsens shared many of their experiences and decisions with us. I learned from him that such sharing is a characteristic of great men.

"One day, for example, he told me he wanted my opinion regarding the establishment of a new sanitarium and hospital at Hinsdale, not far from Chicago, so we went out to see a Mr. Kimball, the owner of the property. That day Dr. Paulsen decided to recommend the establishment of Hinsdale Sanitarium, presently one of Illinois' finest medical institutions. I watched with great interest, eagerly learned as Dr. Paulsen, the physician, became Dr. Paulsen the promoter, skillfully raising funds to establish that badly needed hospital. Ultimately, and inevitably, he moved his 'Life-boat Mission' there. Much as I admired the great physician and his noble efforts to rehabilitate his derelicts, I knew that surgery and prevention of disease would occupy my life."

IV

YOUNG SURGEON AT WORK

ONE DAY while Miller was still serving his internship, there came into his office a man whose face was grossly misshapen with a saddle nose. His nostrils came out just above his lips but his nose was flat to his face—a terrible disfigurement. He was so anxious to have something done about it that he would risk almost anything. He expressed hope that the surgeon might "graft skin from some place else and build me up a nose."

Unfortunately, noses are not built up that way. But the young doctor's experimental bent came into play. He studied a method by which he might inject paraffin wax under the skin of what nose the man had to see if he could produce something resembling a normal profile. There were many risks involved. What if he should fail? He talked over his plan with the patient, who quickly agreed to it. The poor fellow was ready for anything, even death, rather than to go on the way he was.

The procedure can best be described in Miller's own words: "First, we injected paraffin under the skin of the man's arm at a point where we could subsequently cut it out without any serious damage or pain. We wanted to be sure that the tissue would grow into the paraffin and organize itself so that if the paraffin later melted the tissue would not flatten out again. After several weeks we were convinced that it would work. In the process we had to invent a special needle, determine the melting point of the wax, and develop other technical angles to ensure success.

"It was necessary to loosen his skin so that there would not be too much tension in blanching of the skin, cutting off circulation. If circulation were cut off, gangrene would set in and a raw ulcer would be the result, leaving the fellow even worse than he had been in the first place. So we started by massaging his nose to loosen the skin. Then day by day we injected bits of paraffin until the nose was built. He may not have won a Mr. America contest, but his nose was no longer a cause of concern."

The experiment was reported in the *Bulletin* of the American Medical Missionary College, showing pictures taken from the beginning to the end of the process. The thrill of this success in his first medical-research venture strengthened in Harry Miller a native genius for invention, and turned the idle curiosity of childhood into a wholesome inquisitiveness which in the years ahead would be dedicated to service for his fellow men and his God.

On another occasion a patient was admitted to Battle Creek Sanitarium with scabs covering his face and extending down onto his body. His condition grew so bad and the odor so strong that Dr. Paulsen told Miller he would have to discharge the man, or all the rest of the patients would leave. But Harry Miller had become attached to the desperately sick fellow, and pleaded with Paulsen to let the man stay, on the ground that this was a particularly interesting case which even the specialists did not understand. The man grew steadily weaker. Cavities filled with black, bloody serum were developing all over his body. Miller called in the best skin specialist he could find.

"Why this man has leprosy," the specialist said.

"Don't tell a soul," Miller begged him. "If anybody else, including Dr. Paulsen, found out that there was a leper in the institution, it would mean no patients, no nurses, no helpers." Somehow he could not believe that the dermatologist's diagnosis was correct.

Finally, the man died. The hapless Miller called in Dr. Newton Evans, the pathologist, and Dr. Frank Otis, the bacteriologist, both at Battle Creek. They in turn called Dr. Oliver Ormsby, later one of the nation's top dermatology authors. Dr. Ormsby was an assistant to Dr. James N. Hyde and Dr. Frank H. Montgomery, leading specialists and writers on skin diseases. It was soon found that the little black, bloody pustules were not only on the skin but in every organ in the body. When Dr. Otis made his test he discovered that they were due to a black blastomycetes fungus.

The doctors tested the serum from these pustules on guinea pigs and monkeys and learned that the man had not had a skin disease at all. He had died from a generalized systemic infection due to the fungus. Hyde and Montgomery financed further study in laboratory work on the fungus, sending specimens of the tissues to leading pathologists at the principal universities and medical schools.

The report on this case by Harry Miller and Oliver Ormsby nearly filled the May, 1903, issue of the *Journal of Dermatology.* They had proved that the blastomycetes, until then regarded as causing only a skin infection, was far more dangerous than had been supposed. For Harry Miller the principal lesson was that every symptom should be carefully investigated. Not if he could help it would he ever treat a symptom without going into the real cause. "Perhaps the greatest thing I learned from Dr. John Harvey Kellogg and Dr. David Paulsen was the importance of preventive medicine," says Dr. Miller. "They taught that if disease can be prevented, then it doesn't have to be cured. People have a thousand habits that cut their lives short—overeating, inactivity, and indulgence in such poisons as tobacco, narcotics, and alcohol. I also learned the value of pain. I found that it gave a message that reformation of some kind was needed."

Miller's association with the distinguished physicians led him to a determination to carry the gospel of preventive medicine to the world. He correctly foresaw that the day would come when peoples of foreign lands would develop their own therapeutic medical skills and would welcome from other countries only those physicians who could teach them how to keep from becoming sick.

The young surgeon and anatomy teacher was made instructor in dermatology at Rush Medical College where he had been a student the year before. Simultaneously, he held skin-disease clinics at Chicago's Hebrew Hospital, taught in the field of eye, ear, nose, and throat, instructed in anatomy, and was assistant professor in surgery at American Medical Missionary College under Dr. W. B. Holden.

A series of highly successful surgical ventures marked Miller as the one to succeed Holden when the latter left American Medical Missionary College to head a hospital in Portland, Oregon. Miller was not yet twenty-four, and this early fulfillment of his ambitions was frightening. He studied harder than ever, and with good reason. Doctors throughout Illinois and Michigan were calling him in on their most difficult cases. One of these involved a farmer in northern Illinois.

Dr. Miller, together with a nurse and a helper, took a train to the appointed place, where the local doctor met them at the station and took them to the farmer's home. The man was in great distress with a badly irritated bladder. Dr. Miller examined him with great care, hoping to avoid an operation under the circumstances. But surgery was the only answer. He inquired about a hospital. There was none; he would have to operate right there in the house. The young surgeon had removed cataracts and had performed all manner of eye, ear, nose, and throat surgery, but this was his first major case of general surgery, and in a farmer's kitchen! The family physician gave the anesthetic. Omar Grantham, a male nurse, stood by with the instruments.

How could one ever get those stones out of the bladder without cutting it wide? A picture of genius in simplicity, Miller took a teaspoon from the kitchen drawer, bent it to the desired shape, and sterilized it. Then from the bladder of the stricken man he scooped out a large quantity of stones. He inserted a tube for drainage and closed up the incision. Leaving Grantham to care for the patient, Miller boarded his train, deeply concerned.

That night, tossing sleeplessly, he told himself: "This is the first man I have slain." The next day the nurse telegraphed that the man was distended with a great deal of gas. Had he punctured and contaminated the peritoneal cavity, wondered the doctor. There were no antibiotics then, and an infection would undoubtedly mean death. He wired Grantham to keep him closely informed—and he prayed. The next day the nurse sent encouraging word. The patient had passed the gas and his temperature was practically normal. "I thanked God as gratefully for that recovery as I had earnestly prayed before the incision," Dr. Miller says. "Without Him, my surgery through the years would not have amounted to much."

There was little hospitalization in those days. Doctors traveled from home to home. Often, Miller would have to boil the instruments on the kitchen stove, give the anesthetic himself, and operate by battery light. The business angle was reminiscent of the local appliance store—one set of tonsils for ten dollars, two for fifteen dollars, and five dollars for each additional set in the family. In the light of present-day medicine this seems almost barbaric, but it is from these medical pioneers that we have gained our knowledge.

During those years, Chicago was the best place for medical training in eye, ear, nose, and throat diseases. Miller studied under some of the world's leading surgeons. One of these was Dr. Oliver

Tydings, the man who developed the Tydings' Snare for taking out tonsils. Miller had been having trouble with his tonsils, and one day after finishing his study under Tydings he asked the surgeon to remove them. Tydings consented, and operated without anesthetic, not an unusual procedure in those days. Moreover Harry, although he ordinarily operated with anesthetic, wanted to prove to himself that he could "take it."

Tydings placed the snare over the tonsil and tightened the wire as usual before pulling the tonsil out. But as he tightened down, the wire broke, squeezing the tonsil with excruciating pain. Finally he grabbed hold of the broken wire and caught the end with an instrument, pulling sufficiently to cut the base of the tonsil. Miller was ready to call it quits, but Dr. Tydings was determined.

"They really made you tough, but we will see that it doesn't happen with the next one," he assured his patient, adding his apology for the pain. But wire in those days was not annealed, and the same thing happened with the second tonsil. Never was Miller more glad that man was not created with three tonsils.

As soon as the ordeal was over Miller picked up a little sputum cup and headed for the nearest car stop. "I'm sure I must have been a spectacle," he recalls, "as I climbed on the downtown streetcar and dizzily rode up Chicago's Wabash and College Grove Avenues with that little box almost constantly at my mouth. That was a miserable night." Nevertheless, the next day he went to work, and somehow the throat healed.

Those days were a far cry from the tonsillectomies today where the patient is first observed, his bleeding and coagulation time checked, a local or general anesthetic given, and the painless operation completed with a day or two in the hospital for follow-up medical care.

V

SLOW BOAT TO CHINA

DR. MILLER was walking to the anatomy laboratory with Stella Houser, one of his older students, when she inquired about his plans for the future, following the completion of his internship. As a personable, dedicated former secretary to the Foreign Mission Board of the Seventh-day Adventist Church she was constantly on the lookout for possible missionaries.

"I think I'll continue with surgery and teaching," he answered.

"Why?"

"You know, I think it would be a wonderful thing if you and your wife would go to China," she said earnestly and with a smile.

Miller had thought vaguely of an excursion to Mexico or Australia sometime, but China had never entered his mind. Now, Stella Houser's suggestion followed him wherever he went. He talked it over casually with Maude. There was nothing specific holding them in the United States, she agreed. It might be an interesting change. And then suddenly questions tumbled over one another. Was there a Divine Plan behind all of this? What would it mean for their lives? What had they to offer to the people of China? What was China really like? Typical Americans that they were, they knew only that China had two cities, Peking and Shanghai, and that it produced Chinese laundrymen.

Miller talked to his former roommate Arthur Selmon, whose fiancée, Bertha, was also a physician.

"Why not!" Selmon approved enthusiastically, and with little hesitation he and Bertha volunteered to go along. Two nurses, Carrie Erickson and Charlotte Simpson, also wanted to go. The idea was snowballing. Yet, it was one thing to decide to go to China, and quite another thing to get there. None of the group had more than a few cents apiece.

When they told Stella Houser that the six of them were ready to go, she was delighted and quickly passed the word on to the secretary of the mission board. The sad news came back: "You are needed, but the board has no funds to send you." If they were to go, they would have to find their own way, their own money, their own transportation.

China nevertheless became their goal and the subject of much study. Tackling it like a seventh-grade social-studies class, they wrote letters to missionaries in China to find out all they could. They bought a mission book entitled *Chinese Characteristics,* and studied about J. Hudson Taylor, pioneer Methodist missionary of the China Inland Mission. Their vision and ambitions grew. Even though they were going as doctors, they would need Christian literature. It turned out that they would have to print it themselves. That meant finding a printing press. The more they learned about Chinese characters and the complex language, the more prohibitive the task became. Without the support of the mission board—except for credentials—the undertaking was going to require more perseverance and sacrifice than they had anticipated. Doubts set in like ugly sores. During those days they spent a lot of time on their knees. They wanted to be certain that they were on the right track.

When Dr. John Harvey Kellogg learned of their plans, he arrived at Chicago from Battle Creek, determined to dissuade them from what he considered a foolhardy move. There were, he said, high stations awaiting them in a number of medical schools and hospitals. He was a persuasive man, but the needs of China stood out in stark relief against the attractive alternative he proposed. It was a heart-rending decision to part with Dr. Kellogg, a decision clouded with occasional forebodings about the future in a country that had been a graveyard for many well-meaning missionaries before them.

A number of people promised financial help, and the missionaries-to-be felt reassured by unmistakable answers to their prayers. One day, for example, they prayed specifically for help to find a printing press if they were supposed to go, for they knew it was a "must." The next day Miller went to the Miehle Printing Press Company in Chicago.

"What kind of power is available in China?" the company president asked the young physician in practical fashion.

"The only kind of power I know of is hand and foot power—pumping a treadle or turning a wheel," he answered.

"We have nothing but power cylinder presses. Perhaps you had better go over to Barnhart and Spindler," the executive suggested.

Dr. Miller walked on down the street, found the office, and asked to see the manager. After a long wait the secretary said that the manager was too busy that day.

"Come another time," she added. He made an appointment for the next day, arrived before the plant was open, and sat on the steps waiting for the door to be unlocked. Once he was in the office there was another long wait before the secretary asked the nature of his business.

"Believe me, she protected her boss well," Harry said later to a friend. "I didn't dare tell her until I saw the manager himself, and I was beginning to doubt whether I ever would see him. But finally I was given entree, and I told him my story."

The manager promised to talk the matter over with his officers and to let Miller know the result the next day, although there was little assurance in his voice. The young physicians remained in prayer that night. The next day the manager offered them a printing press and asked how they wanted it shipped. Miller told him to send it to Montgomery Ward, which was handling all of their equipment.

It was a joyful group that gathered together that evening. "We all knelt in thanksgiving," Dr. Miller recalls, "But this was only one of many evidences that He was opening the way. We were certain that He wanted us to go and would bless our work. The manager of the printing press company hadn't even asked what church was represented. Nor had he established the fact that we were appointed missionaries. When we arrived in China later, we found that he not only had sent along a fine Franklin press, but had included a complete font of English type, which was far more than we had ever thought of."

One by one the elements of the puzzle began to fit into place. A typewriter was given by a relative, and there were personal effects from friends. The Mueller Instrument Company in Chicago contributed surgical instruments and an operating table. Miller's home conference of Ohio, and the Iowa Conference from which Selmon came, agreed to pay their transportation and to contribute a small allowance for the first year. They were to receive about seven dollars a week for each family. Out of this they would pay the nurses. The conferences also bestowed ministerial credentials and, late in 1903, sent the dedicated little band on its way, ordained to the medical ministry of China.

For three days and four nights the *te-click te-clack* of train wheels sounded in the ears of the six missionaries as they rode to Vancouver on the first lap of their long journey. They were exhausted when they arrived at the port city, and with their motley assortment of baggage, they made their way to a hotel. They soon found that the cheapest ocean transportation available was third-class—actually steerage—on the Canadian Pacific's *Empress of India*. It cost precisely one hundred dollars apiece.

The ship belied its name. It was a small vessel, anything but regal. The young missionaries' rooms were down in its bowels, just over the rumbling propeller shaft.

That voyage remains a vivid memory in Dr. Miller's mind: "On the afternoon of October 3, 1903, as the *Empress* moved away from the pier and down Puget Sound, we moved up to the deck, confident in the beginning of our great adventure. We paraded up and down the ship assuring each other that we would all be good sailors. None of us felt the least bit sick. It hadn't occurred to us that we were still in inland waters, level and friendly as a garden pond. Except for the vibration of the engines there was little sense of motion.

"We made a brief stop at Victoria and then headed out into the deep, cocky as ever. By this time we were all in bed, and the boat was beginning to rock. If it had just rocked one way it wouldn't have been so bad, but it was rocking all ways and always. A terrible sensation came over me. Selmon and I were in the same airtight cabin, and the four women in another. Soon we were so sick that neither of us could even get up to check on the women.

" 'Surely this will let up,' we comforted one another. But it only became worse. The sicker we became, the more dehydrated we were because we couldn't eat or drink a thing. Nor could we sit up or even get out of the cabin. And I, the cockiest one, was the worst of all. There were no effective seasickness remedies in those days, although there was a plethora of fruitless ideas on how to prevent seasickness.

"Finally, after four days and nights of lying there, turning and twisting in agony and desperation, I consented to the urging of the women and Selmon to go up to the deck. With unspeakable weakness I half crawled, and was half lifted, up the gangway to the deck, where I sprawled like one of Dr. Paulsen's drunks. The fresh ocean air was exhilarating and the ship's personnel attentive and kind, but my self-confidence was so far gone that I didn't leave the cabin or deck chair for the next nine days, except for one excursion to the dining room, before arriving at Yokohama. My first impression of that oriental city was that all of its streets and buildings were rocking up and down, and I walked gingerly to meet its movements."

Dr. Miller still remembers the vow he made at that time: "I'm going to China and stay there all my life. I'm never going back to America again. I'll die before going through a siege of seasickness like that." Grim as it was, he admits it probably was one of the most salutary educational experiences of his life.

But Harry Miller was no seer. In the future he would complete scores of ocean crossings by ship and airplane. His medical ministry was to carry him into all parts of the United States and to more than fifty nations of the world in one of the widest-ranging and most significant medical practices in history.

VI

FROM MUFTI TO MAO TZE
AND QUEUE

JAPAN AT THE TURN of the century was in no respect a disappointment to the adventurers. Those were the days when the foreigner
thought of Japan in terms of the ricksha, and the rickshas were
welcome conveyances indeed for the weakened and weary
travelers. For a few cents they let themselves be hauled all over
Yokohama, even though they joked with each other about being
carted around like babies.

The most significant experience in their early travels was the
realization that they had friends in every port. The precious
fellowship of the missionary brotherhood soon dawned upon
them. Kobe followed Yokohama. There they were met by Dr.
and Mrs. Sheridan Lockwood, classmates from American Medical
Missionary College days, with whom they spent an evening.

Miller never forgot Myrtle Lockwood's cooking, the first satisfying meal in more than two weeks for the half-starved six. The
Lockwoods were so happy to see friends from America that they
did not mind being eaten out of house and home. Yet that meal
was important in a far larger sense than that of fellowship and
good cooking. That was the night Miller was introduced to the
soybean.

41

He was particularly impressed with an entree called "tofu loaf," which he learned was a cheese from the soybean. A common and inexpensive oriental food, it made an unusually wholesome dish, rich in protein. It aroused Miller's curiosity intensely from the standpoint of preventive medicine, but there was little time for investigation then. That was to come later.

Suddenly there seemed to be an uneasiness among the happy group talking over old times.

"I've a feeling we'd better go back to the boat," Harry suggested to his friends.

"But it's only nine-thirty, and the boat doesn't leave until midnight. Why be in such a hurry?"

The Lockwoods wanted to keep their friends with them as long as possible. Nevertheless, the travelers were not taking any chances, and it was well that they did not.

Racing down to the pier, they found that the ship, far out in the harbor, was already pulling anchor. Commandeering a sampan, and waving and yelling frantically, they managed to catch the attention of a passenger. A rope ladder was thrown down, and, silhouetted against the harbor lights, the greenhorns made their shaky ascent, more concerned about getting to China than about the risk of the deep water below. Ten minutes later and they would have been left behind.

Down Japan's Inland Sea the *Empress* moved with all the grace of a majestic swan in a sheltered cove. Suspicious of this tranquility and heeding the lesson from their experience in Puget Sound, the travelers stayed close to the fresh air of the open decks, and were happily surprised to find that even the swells of the Yellow Sea did not seriously challenge their equilibrium.

The significance of the name of these oriental waters became obvious as the deep blue of the Pacific changed to muddy yellow. For the waters of the Yangtze River discolor the ocean one hundred fifty miles out with the yellow mud spewed from its mouth at Shanghai.

Although ocean-going vessels traveled as far as six hundred miles up the big river to Hankow, the little group of missionary adventurers disembarked at Shanghai into the arms of J. N. Anderson, China pioneer, who took them to the nearby Seventh-day Baptist compound. The hospitality there was typical of the friendliness which existed among the missionaries sent out by various denominational mission boards. Pastor David Herbert Davis, of the compound, was at the time translating the Bible into Chinese. Before long the newcomers began to realize the import of Davis' work. They developed a healthy respect for one of the missionary's greatest obstacles, the language barrier.

Then it was "on to Hankow" for the group. There they were met by veteran worker Erik Pilquist, a Swedish Adventist missionary with the British and Foreign Bible Society. He had been assigned to take them to the interior of China. But first the two doctors had to go to the American consulate to register and to pay their respects to the consul general. To the young idealists he was an amazing character, treating his visitors to one long, cynical harangue:

"Why do you young men want to come over here? Are you going to waste away your lives in this miserable country? Why don't you apply for a place in the State Department? The State is needing young men like you over here—to learn the language and work your way up in diplomatic circles. Who knows, maybe you'll become ambassador to China, or some other place? You might as well be buried as to go to the interior. No one will ever hear of you."

His admonition to "learn the language" was ironic. He could speak hardly a word of Chinese, although he considered himself fluent in the language. Long years before, Chinese sailors had imported a phrase in pidgin-Spanish: "You no savvy?" Chinese helpers used it frequently when they wanted to ascertain whether Americans understood them. That expression was about the extent of the consul general's "Chinese" vocabulary.

He called in one of his Chinese helpers and spoke to him in English. The Chinese, of course, did not understand him. Then the consul, obviously irritated, demanded, "You no savvy?"

The Chinese looked at him blankly.

"Look at that," the consul said, "he doesn't even understand his own language."

The experience provided the newcomers a strong impetus to learn the language—and soon. They were encouraged later to find that that consul was not typical of United States officials abroad.

They would need some Chinese clothing, Pilquist pointed out, because there were no laundrymen in the interior to take care of foreign shirts and collars.

No laundrymen! This was distressing, for they had spent many precious pennies on clothes before leaving America, under the impression that Chinese laundrymen would be everywhere. But, resigned to their disappointment, the men purchased long-sleeved gowns in a variety of colors. Shoes were harder to find. Their feet were just too big. It was even worse for the women, because many of the Chinese women in those days bound their feet. Missionary Pilquist modestly demurred at helping Carrie Erickson and Charlotte Simpson select their clothes, with the result that they returned from the shops with a strange assortment of clothing suitable for elderly women.

As they walked down the road after being outfitted, first Selmon, then Miller heard a rip. They were not used to walking in gowns, and already the seams were beginning to split, tearing more with each awkward stride. Their dignified Swedish companion turned his head repeatedly in uncontrollable mirth. Had it not been so utterly comical they would have been insulted.

Adjusting to China included more than learning the Chinese language and becoming adept at walking in long robes. There was the matter of the queue, or pigtail. This unusual custom—known to Confucius—traced back ultimately to filial piety. The custom declined with the passage of time, but the Manchus, on coming to power in 1644, revived the queue—requiring the Chinese to wear it as a symbol of submission. The tyrannical old Empress Dowager of the Manchu Government, still in power when the adventurous six from America reached China, demanded "loyalty by pigtail." Each Chinese man had to shave his head, leaving only a patch of hair toward the back, which was plaited to hang down in a queue, and often was artificially lengthened. Crowning this strange coiffure was a *mao tze*—a blockish beanie, or skullcap.

Should they? Dared they? Yes, decided the doctors, determined to be as like the Chinese as possible. And so they shaved their heads and put on pigtail wigs, matching the color to that of their own shorn locks as closely as possible—not an easy accomplishment in black-haired China.

Miller succeeded so well in his desire to appear Chinese that he later had a problem of another sort—to appear American! There came a time, after his own hair had grown long enough to make a pigtail, when Miller wanted to view the first of a series of sham battles between the armies of Generals Yüan Shih-k'ai and Chang Tse-chang. No ordinary Chinese would be permitted to witness such a military demonstration. To be allowed on the military train—the only available transportation—Miller had to look like a foreigner. The question was, what to do about the queue.

The doctor solved that problem by coiling his long braid of hair on top of his head and covering it with a *mao tze*. Hoping to make it less obvious, he topped that with an American hat which he removed when indoors, leaving the skullcap on. This worked fairly well among friends who were acquainted with his Chinese habits but created an embarrassing moment when he called at the Methodist mission in Peking, prior to boarding the military train.

He found Dr. George Davis Lowry, head of the mission, as hospitable as other Methodists whom he knew in the south. Conscious of the rolled-up queue under his skullcap, the doctor tried, unsuccessfully, to refuse a warm invitation to dine at the mission.

Sitting down to dinner with the Lowry family and their guests, Miller found the children all around the table staring at the *mao tze* on his head. The blessing was said and the meal begun, but one little boy, his food untouched, never moved his eyes from the skullcap.

Finally, turning to his father, he asked:

"Daddy, why doesn't the man take off his hat?"

Dr. Lowry tried to quiet him with a smile and a comment on another subject, but in the suddenly uneasy atmosphere around the table, the boy turned to Dr. Miller.

"Mister, why don't you take off your hat at the table?"

The Lowrys and their guests broke the tension with a good laugh, and Dr. Miller explained that in Shangtsai he lived and dressed like a Chinese, and was wearing foreign clothes just to attend the military affair.

When Dr. Miller arrived at the railway terminal he met two other Americans who wanted to ride the train to the demonstration point. The three of them approached one of the majors standing by the train and asked his permission to board. Eyeing his chief nearby, the major roared with a great show of authority:

"This is a military train, not for civilian passengers."

The Americans backed away, embarrassed, still hoping, however, to get on the train just as it started. At the call of "All Aboard" an officer came racing toward them. It was the same major.

"Jump on! Jump on! It does not matter." It was quite clear that he had wanted to put them on all along, but had not dared to while his chief was still there. Miller had passed as an American, coiled queue and all.

Dr. Miller still smiles when he thinks of that time, but he says, with genuine feeling: "Queue or no queue, it is my considered opinion that if more missionaries and government emissaries would empathize with the people instead of treating them as second-class citizens and insisting on the 'American way of life,' the Christian gospel and the truths of democracy might gather considerably more momentum than is apparent now."

Peking, the scene of Miller's later American-turned-Chinese-turned-American adventure was, in 1903, furthest from his thoughts. When Harry and Arthur donned their pigtails for the first time, their destination was Hsintsai, and it beckoned with growing urgency. In those days the Belgian-run railway extended only to Sinyang, one hundred and fifty miles north of Hankow. For some unknown reason, the Belgians habitually waited until the last minute to open the ticket windows. Perhaps they enjoyed the mad scramble it caused. When Pilquist and the six Americans arrived at the Hankow terminal they were literally swallowed up in the shoving, pushing throng that eventually made its way onto the old third-class coaches. As the engine wheezed, belched, and creaked along, they jerked accommodatingly with it, poking their heads through the crowd for a peek at the countryside. In the fields, farmers plowed behind their water buffaloes with crude implements such as have been used for millenniums. Eight hours later, they were jostled off at Sinyang.

Pilquist led his party to one of the local hotels for the night. They entered the building through the kitchen. Stooping and dodging to avoid the blackest of soot at every hand, the Americans betrayed through their facial expressions an amazement bordering on horror. The dirt-floored kitchen contained one big kettle suspended over a fire fueled by cornstalks, cane refuse, and rice straw. In the stuffy room, which had no chimney, the cooks were constantly wiping their faces, noses, and eyes irritated by the smoke. Moments later they would use the same towels on their utensils. During the long trip, the hungry travelers had been anticipating more of the foreign food they had grown to like, but not one of the six ate a bite that night. Pilquist dined alone.

With stomachs empty, the Americans climbed wearily to their "rooms," which were merely sections of one large room separated by thin rice-straw mats. The beds were bamboo racks with wooden blocks for pillows, but even those looked inviting. Spreading out their bedding, they quickly "fell in." However, they had not reckoned with the hotelkeeper, who had generously arranged to honor his distinguished guests—Americans were a rarity in Sinyang—by providing a serenade through the night. In came the musicians with their giraffe-necked banjos and a half-dozen other instruments, from which they drew forth an unending flow of moaning tones in a minor key.

No sooner had the travelers finally fallen asleep in the early hours of the morning, than they were awakened by a loud and ferocious chatter in front of the hotel. A veritable hive of coolies was bargaining with Pilquist: to run the wheelbarrows, to carry the sedan chairs, to transport equipment. The happy impression of the Americans that their destination lay only a few hours' journey distant was shattered by their discovery that it would be three days before they reached Hsintsai—three long days, filled with the roughest, harshest kind of travel they had ever known. How little they actually knew about China!

Dr. Miller still remembers clearly every detail of that first trip into the interior of China. "Eventually," he recalls, "we *had* to fill our stomachs. And how we wished we had had the sense to eat in the comparative refinement of the hotel. If we could only have looked at the noodles instead of the people who prepared them, things would have been a lot easier. The flavor was actually good, judging by the smell. Every few steps, it seemed, the food vendors would move into step with our coolie carriers and chatter up at us, obviously explaining the superiority of their particular foods. Sleeves rolled up to their elbows, paste and flour all over their unwashed garments, they rinsed off their chopsticks with grimy hands in water that must have come from a sump. All of this was just too much for us. For the entire first day we went without food.

"If we had hoped for any respite from this situation, we had a lot to learn, as indeed nearly all missionaries soon find out, for they seldom have the larger budgets afforded the diplomats and businessmen who are overseas. We had not traveled eight hours that day, but fourteen. And that night there were no separations in the big room where we slept. By then nobody seemed to care much, except that once in a while we would wonder why we hadn't stayed in Hankow and started some medical work there instead of hopefully moving into the interior where there wouldn't be other English-speaking people for miles and days. Maybe the consul had not been so wrong.

"That rare modern American tourist who ventures off the beaten path and finds himself among the country people of the Orient will have some idea about the confusion that surrounded us every time we were trotted through a village. By the hundreds and sometimes by the thousands they would press in upon us, six white-faced 'Chinese,' about as comfortable in our oriental paraphernalia as a Kentucky backwoodsman in white tie and tails.

"However, we felt that we had a lot to be thankful for. The days were unusually sunny and clear for November, and we were still in good health. As a matter of fact, we were probably more optimistic than the occasion warranted."

That night as the weary little group staggered into the big room that was to be their overnight haven, Pilquist asked:

"Do you know what those people were saying to you out there today?"

No, no one knew.

"Well, they were calling you 'foreign devils' and 'foreign dogs,'" he continued without any particular emotion. "You will have to get used to that. Affection over here isn't automatic. You must earn your way into their hearts. You were a novelty to the people in Sinyang last night, but in most places foreigners are not tolerated now."

Pilquist then proceeded to explain to them some recent Chinese history. Americans, like other foreigners, were still living in the shadows of the Boxer Rebellion. The encroachment of Western nations and the undeniable need for reform in China had produced widespread discontent by the turn of the century. Retaliatory measures against the foreign powers were almost inevitable, and one Government decree called for revival of the village-militia system. Secret societies developed within it, one being *I Ho T'uan*—Righteous Harmony Bands or Righteous Harmony Fists—commonly called Boxers. They were bent on ousting foreigners from China's northern Provinces, and the bloody climax to their drive came at Peking in 1900 after the Western countries had tried, without success, to send additional troops into the city. The Manchu Empress Dowager ordered all foreigners killed. Many missionaries ("foreign devils") and thousands of Chinese Christians ("secondary foreign devils") were massacred. The total result was to lessen the power of the despotic Empress Dowager and to make more secure Western control in China.

The offended nations made stringent demands on the Chinese Government. The mayor of each city was held personally responsible for the safety of the foreigners residing in his city. By 1903, when Pilquist and his party were heading for Hsintsai, foreigners still were not allowed to go outside the city walls without a military escort, so the inevitable soldiers were accompanying the missionary group. Neither foreigner nor Chinese liked the situation, but there was no choice. If a foreigner wanted to make a trip to another town he had to have an escort of at least two soldiers.

For weapons the soldiers carried guns or swords, the guns being American Civil War surplus. The Chinese Government had bought fifty thousand of them from an enterprising American trader. The fact that few of them were in working order did not seem to matter. They looked like guns, and that was sufficient. One soldier would carry a musket and the other one a sword—and the swords were sharp.

That evening the six Americans did a lot of thinking, coming at last to the realization that they were not adventurers. They were missionaries, and the price of their calling might be higher than they had imagined. Sobering reality had swallowed up any romantic daydreams, but out of their hunger and exhaustion rose, inexplicably, a new firmness of purpose and a greater eagerness to serve.

VII

THE PENNILESS VIP

HARRY MILLER, outdoors ahead of the others the next morning, watched the wizened old Chinese edging his way along the wall, head down, apparently searching for something, though for what no one seemed to know or care. Whatever his wants, they had little relation to time. The hands of the coolie class were heavy with time, miserable, hungry, deathly time. Their lives were an eternal night. Yet few would ever give voice to the quiet desperation of their souls.

Whether out of pride or fear, or because of the steel bands of tradition which bound the oriental mind; whether babies, youth, or aged—they suffered and died. They passed in silence. Not by hundreds nor by thousands, but by unnumbered generations, which seemed linked only by the chains of oblivion. Miller's rugged young heart ached compassionately as he watched the old man. He had seen so many others—just like that man. He longed, through his healing hands, to bring them hope.

Suddenly it was time for the morning meal—the others were up —and then to be on their way again. The end of the trek was in sight.

On the last day of the journey, November 5, 1903, the sun rose brightly. "After morning prayer," says the doctor, "we girded our courage to make the last twenty miles over the narrow, winding paths, through hostile villages, for we were anxious to be settled at Hsintsai. Before we left the inn we celebrated our new courage with a meal of long, fried Chinese pretzels, and water that we boiled. I still remember raking the leaves out of that water before boiling it, and letting the mud settle before drinking it. Even the pretzels somehow began to taste good."

And so, after three days of riding, rocking, and shuffling along, and occasionally halting that the physicians might minister to passing sick or wounded, leader Pilquist and his tired party sighted the gates of Hsintsai illuminated in the distance by the rays of the setting sun. By that time the travelers were prepared for anything. Surely their new headquarters could not be much worse than the lodgings of the last three nights. Nor were they, thanks to the love of the missionary family serving there. As a matter of fact, the Selmons, the two nurses, and Maude and Harry each had apartments to themselves; at least, they were apartments to the grateful wayfarers, the silver linings of the clouds they had just passed through.

But they had no visions of grandeur. They knew they would have to live on the food of the land. That meant rice and noodles, a few peanuts, and syrup made from malted wheat. With few apologies to their solicitous hosts, the newcomers ate like famished orphans that first night. Indeed, their spirits were so high after the feast, that a passer-by might have wondered if the malted grain had not turned to alcohol. It had not. The exultation was really a sobering one. Before the evening was over there was a thanksgiving service which would have matched that of the Pilgrims.

The group at Hsintsai made up an earnest little American island in the vast oriental ocean. The only way to navigate that sea was to learn the Chinese language, but who in that outlying area could teach Chinese to Americans? Finally, the new missionaries

found an old professor who could speak no English. This might
have proved a fortunate handicap, except that he knew little
about teaching. His pupils would point to a Chinese character, and
he would pronounce it. Then they would try to imitate him.

Around and around it went, but not much learning came out.
Competition was keen to see who could read and write the most
Chinese characters, but nobody was learning how to speak the
language. Nobody, that is, except Carrie Erickson. She soon tired
of the professorial merry-go-round, and spent more and more
time at the local market. There she would play with the children,
listen to the people, and oftentimes try to ask them questions.
She did not learn many characters, but before long her associates
discovered that she was the only one who could make herself
understood. They all came to rely on her for shopping, and several
of the group, heeding her example, soon came to depend less upon
the old scholar and more upon the educators of the market place.

It is the nature of missionaries learning a language to look for
any available short cut; but when the Millers were told that
putting on Chinese costumes would be a great help in learning
the language, they could not take it seriously! Harry thoroughly
agreed with Wesley, who was reputed to have said that the Devil
invented the Chinese language to keep missionaries away. The
military restrictions consequent upon the Boxer Rebellion kept
the foreigners so close to home, however, that they were left with
no excuse for not studying.

It was a good thing that Carrie Erickson was as intrepid as
she was, for marketing was a daily necessity. The Chinese lived
one day at a time, a practice typical over the Orient. This was not
only because they were very poor but also because food spoiled
easily and could not be kept long. The wheat, for example, had to
be washed because it was flailed out on the ground. Its product
was a moist flour which would not keep well in the warm climate.
It did not take long for the new missionaries to learn the meaning
of "Give us *this day* our daily bread."

Before they adopted the local custom of daily marketing, the missionaries had established a reputation in the community for having enormous appetites. The Chinese merchants had reported around the neighborhood the large quantities of food the foreigners had purchased, for at first they had bought almost all the peanuts or sweet potatoes the vendor had. After they adopted the day-to-day market plan, the quaint Chinese salutation acquired new meaning for them. "*Hwei koh er tsi ma?*" they would repeat in greeting—"Are you able to live over the day?"

As time passed, travel became less restricted for foreigners, and the military escort was no longer required. Occasional trips to Hankow provided welcome release to the missionaries from the binding routine of language study. In northern China, travel was ordinarily by oxcart; but the Americans usually preferred to walk, letting the carts carry the luggage.

Over the years Dr. Miller has made numberless journeys in China. One, at least, he will never forget. "Early in the spring of 1904 Arthur Selmon and I headed for Hankow to pick up some provisions and to receive some freight that had been sent from America," Miller tells the story. "We padded ourselves, Chinese style, against the cold weather and set out on the three-day journey, which we made mostly by foot.

"Not the least important was our mail, with news from home, and our American checks, which we cashed into lump silver. We decided it would be cheaper for us to rent a raft and take our supplies home by river than to hire oxcarts for travel via land. So, after our rail ride from Hankow to Sinyang, we moved our things to some bamboo rafts. This way, we figured, we would not only save money but could sleep on the rafts at night while they were being poled up the shallow river by the boatmen.

"The trip proved to be tedious and dangerous. Whenever the water was too shallow to float the raft, a couple of men would move on ahead and make a little dam of sand to raise the water in the shallow places. The boatmen would then push the raft with great vigor to develop enough momentum so that it would slide over the sand into the deeper water and float on.

"After a couple of days of this lazy traveling on the meandering stream, it was decided that I should go ahead by foot with one of the helpers and purchase a shipment of charcoal at the next town. Arthur would remain on the raft with the freight—and the silver. The river was so winding that it was easy for me to far outdistance the boat. Cutting out across country, a coolie and I walked all that night, arriving the next morning at the charcoal market. We soon had the fuel down at the riverbank ready for loading onto the raft. But no raft came.

"After several hours a local official came by with the news that bandits had attacked a raft down the river and that men were hurt. We ran for what must have been several miles until we found the rafts pushed at an odd angle up on the riverbank. Selmon was in great pain with an arm injury, and the Chinese helpers provided a bloody background with gashes on their arms, sides, and faces, and one man's lips were hanging pitifully from his face.

"Robbers had apparently witnessed the silver transaction at Hankow and had followed us. With a number of knives and swords, they had accosted Selmon and the coolies at a time when the raft was nearest the shore. When Arthur and the men pushed the raft away from the bank the bandits waded out and tried to crawl or climb on for the showdown. Using their poles and the stove wood which was piled on the raft, the men threw it and poked at the attackers until they finally went away.

"The most amazing aspect of the whole experience was the loyalty of the coolies, who didn't even know us and who were normally reputed to be deathly afraid of bandits. Again we thanked God, and with Chinese needles and thread, we sewed up the wounds, and trusted to His healing power.

"Just as we were rearranging the freight on our raft in preparation for the rest of the journey, a courier arrived from Pilquist, who by this time had moved to another city. The note said that his wife was very sick. Could we come at once and treat her? Selmon's arm was hurt, possibly fractured. He could not go, so there was nothing for me to do but head for the Pilquist home." Without rest, Miller made his way partly by foot and partly on pony back to find that Mrs. Pilquist was down with a gall bladder attack.

Dr. Miller continues: "She was not in serious condition, however. I quickly prescribed treatment, and left. Arthur and I had agreed that I would be back in twenty-four hours or the raft should leave; if I were not there within the stated time it would be a signal that Mrs. Pilquist was seriously ill. As I started back, the rains descended in full force. Since the only roads were narrow paths between the rice fields, going became extremely difficult. Having gone one direction with me, the courier decided I should know my way back and sent me off alone. It was the first time I had traveled by myself in China."

The tired physician hurried along as rapidly as possible under the circumstances, hoping to reach the raft before it left. But when he arrived at the appointed place, the men were gone. All he had were two copper coins, a dead-tired body, and an empty stomach. He sent a runner to a nearby store to buy some native apricots; but the coolie brought back instead a little bunch of strings. Miller learned later that the words for apricots and strings are much alike, which further emphasized the importance of learning accurately the native tongue.

He was at his wit's end, and too tired to care, when two soldiers appeared suddenly, walking purposefully in his direction. On top of all this trouble was he now going to be arrested? What did they suspect him of? A hundred fearful questions tumbled through his weary mind.

The soldiers marched Miller to the district magistrate where he was carefully questioned. Satisfied that he was simply trying to catch up with the raft, and aware that he was exhausted, the local officials insisted that he rest before he left. They gave him their choicest accommodations, with the best bamboo bed and cotton-filled quilts, and brought him food from the magistrate's table. There he slept gratefully though fitfully, surrounded by opium-smoking guests, his eyes and nostrils stinging from the fumes.

The next morning, to Miller's consternation, the magistrate sent his own sedan chair to take the doctor to the raft. Never before had Harry been treated with so much ceremony. A horseman went before him holding aloft a big red umbrella, which told all who looked on that this was a Very Important Person. Four coolies carried him in the sedan chair, and they were followed by four more coolies trotting along as relief men. Under his seat clanked two strings of copper coins, a thousand coppers to the string. Coins jingling, coolies singing, they proceeded at a great pace, with the alternates moving in for their turns every mile or so without stopping the retinue. Every few miles the horseman would procure food or drink, using a few of the coppers for the purpose.

As pompous as a maharajah on an elephant and suddenly and oddly carefree, Harry Miller found himself reflecting on the unexpected rewards of Christian service. He remembered his book-selling days in Ohio when he had sometimes gone two days without food. He even thought about his first weeks in China when he had frequently been jeered at—"*Yang qui tsu,* the foreign devil." Now here he was, penniless, in a strange territory, with the so-called heathen literally treating him like a magistrate—or a king.

The flamboyant procession made a lasting impression on the startled Arthur Selmon when they came upon him and the raft shortly after noontime. "It was quite a meeting," Dr. Miller recollects. "Those who have experienced uncertainty and the unknown will understand our relief and gratitude. But this adventure convinced us even more that China needed us. The boatmen were among our first patients. They had fought valiantly for us when one would have expected them to turn against us. Was it not a kind of miracle? Except for them our bodies might have been with those of many others, also bandit victims, that we had seen floating down the river."

Despite all they had heard of China's "heathen darkness," Harry Miller and Arthur Selmon were now certain that in China, too, the good far outweighed the bad. "Returning home was always a thrilling occasion," says Dr. Miller. "The heroism of our wives—isolated in almost every respect—was fully known only by heaven." With all the hazards of illness, bandits, and numerous accidents, the women never knew when, or if, the men would return. That evening the reunion of Miller and Selmon with their wives and fellow workers was a festive occasion as they passed out the little treats from America, England, and the Continent, which they had purchased in Hankow. Transcending everything was their abiding gratitude for the guidance and protection of their God.

VIII

STRANGE HORIZONS

WITH UNVOICED APPREHENSION the young workers soberly anticipated the day when they would have to separate. After studying Chinese and working together in Hsintsai for about a year, they decided it was time for each family to form the nucleus of a mission in another city, the centers selected to be twenty to fifty miles apart. Since Harry Miller was responsible for the printing press, he and Maude moved nearer the railroad. By then the Belgians had added another forty miles to the line, so the Millers moved to the walled city of Shangtsai, about twenty miles from the new terminus.

Harry and Maude managed to rent a small group of buildings on the main road, where they could house several helpers, a small print shop, a chapel at the street entrance, and for themselves a bedroom, a tiny study, and a little kitchen. Maude carried out her wifely chores, centered around a Chinese charcoal stove, while Harry made plans to print Christian literature. They also set up dispensary hours, and taught the gospel story as they cured physical ailments.

Thoughts of those early days bring many incidents to Dr. Miller's mind: "I had a lot to learn about putting together a printing plant. First, we had to build a heavy floor and some racks for our type, which meant buying lumber; and that required another trip to Hankow. By this time each of us had had a turn at dysentery and we were more than usually careful about how we ate while traveling. I always took my medicine case along; besides, it doubled for a moneybag." He adds that he was incredibly naïve, as he looks back on it, always hopeful and often confident.

Dr. Miller went to Hankow. After making arrangements for the lumber and replenishing his bag with money as well as medicines, he spread out his bedding roll on top of the railroad car where his lumber had been stacked. That was one night he was going to have some sleep. But in the few moments during which he stepped over to the freight office to pay his bill, someone stole the bedding roll. "Yet it could have been far worse," he says. "Fortunately, I had my medicine case with me, containing the silver from newly cashed checks I had just received from America. There wasn't much sleep that night, shivering up there on top of those green boards."

Thievery was common among the poverty-ridden masses, and quite in keeping with their pragmatic philosophy that if it worked it was all right—nothing was wrong unless you were found out. From childhood the people were taught to evade the law rather than to observe it. "I have oftentimes wondered since which were the more skillful at this technique, the Chinese or my own countrymen," says Dr. Miller.

In reminiscent vein, he continues: "This philosophy often led to humorous experiences. One time my janitor was sweeping the floor and the end of his handle struck the window glass. I knew it was an accident, but glass wasn't easy to secure. I asked him later if he had broken it. He said, 'Oh, no!' I then told him that I had been in the house and had seen him break it. With the most solemn face he replied, 'I didn't do it, the broom handle did it.' Any amount of orating on good living or on the development of religious doctrine in Sabbath sermons, I decided, would not be as effective as a simple Christian example. These people were testing us under every circumstance.

"Sighting the fine load of pine lumber, the Chinese workers praised me on my choice of 'coffin wood.' Pine happened to be their favorite for burial purposes, and the head of each house prided himself on the polished pine coffin he kept as furniture in his home. A visitor would hardly think to leave without complimenting the patriarch of the household on his coffin. I had to guard that wood as if it were gold."

During the stopover in Japan on the outward voyage, Miller had purchased a font of Chinese type. Japan was an industrial nation, so things could be purchased much more cheaply there. There were about three thousand different characters to pigeonhole in the type boxes. The English alphabet can be complicated enough in a type case, but the doctor, without the slightest knowledge of the art of printing and with only a limited knowledge of Chinese at that time, faced a situation many times more complex than any American printer would be apt to meet.

Miller sawed and chipped and planed until he had built a stand for the Franklin press and had completed the racks and cases for the type. His Chinese helpers labeled the boxes and distributed the characters. He congratulated himself that he was about ready to begin, only to discover that he had no ink rollers.

Harry could get along without electricity. He did not even require heat in the icy room. But he did have to have rollers. One trip to Hankow and a dozen sheets of gelatin later, and he had his rollers—fashioned around a roughened core of iron and a form made from tin worked into the shape of a rolling pin. They proved to be excellent rollers.

The next question was, what to use in order to cover them with ink. The Chinese used big flat sandstones, but after working for days trying to grind down the stone, Miller's helpers still left so many rough places that the situation looked impossible. Every time they smoothed the stone to take care of one hole, another soft spot would appear. Finally, in desperation, the doctor flattened out a piece of stove pipe, nailed it to a board, and had an excellent inking stand.

Then the ink rebelled. Miller had decided to work regardless of the freezing weather in the shop. But he had not consulted the ink. It was entirely too thick to use, and could not be thinned with water because it had an oil base. Peanut oil worked well, but when the helpers rolled the ink onto the type and made an impression on the paper, little halos of oil surrounded every character.

Miller suddenly realized that the Chinese must have a similar problem. Nearly every Chinese whom he knew had his own seal, for in the Orient it served as legal signature in lieu of a pen. Harry soon found that they lubricated their ink with castor oil, so down to the apothecary he went. He had never learned this in pharmacy classes at medical school, but it was just what the doctor ordered.

Next, the doctor-turned-printer started down the street to find another helper, for those that he had were already more than busy. Harry found a skinny, half-clothed boy whom he had seen frequently selling matches on the street. The youngster's bright eyes and steady smile were appealing, so the Millers put some more clothes on him and hired him to feed the paper and turn the handle. His name was Chang T'ai-hsing.

Chang taught them still another lesson—that a missionary's first fruits can come from the most unexpected places. During the early months they were all so inexperienced in setting up the forms for the press, and in gathering and distributing the type, that Chang had time on his hands. He spent every spare minute with the writers and proofreaders, and after a while became a typesetter himself. In the process he read himself into the Christian faith and became a highly successful evangelist. About the same time, a printer by the name of Wen Tén-wang joined the concern—and stayed for forty years, until the Communists put the press out of business. Today, his son is one of the owners of the prominent Peking Restaurants in Washington, D.C.

The primitive printing establishment soon had some single-page tracts off the press. The printers then decided to translate and publish some of the more familiar Christian hymns. They all but stood on their heads at times trying to fit the Chinese characters into the rhythm and the tunes.

The next question was, how to sell the little papers; the Millers could not afford to publish them free. They started with the patients in their dispensary, giving the tracts to all, and charging those who could afford it enough extra for their medicine to pay for the paper. One day after a patient had walked out of the dispensary, he turned around and came back, asking how the little paper was to cure his sickness.

The publishers had not anticipated how many people the small tracts and hymns would reach. If a patient could not read, he carried the paper to someone who could. Because reading matter was so scarce, the reader usually gathered several people around him before he read and explained the material. Oftentimes the "scholars" took the paper to the center of the village and stood up on a bench or stool. As quick and sure as iron filings near a magnet, the villagers would press in about the readers, unwittingly making of them preachers of the Christian gospel. The doctor's helpers took a cue from that, and before long colporteurs were selling the primitive gospel literature through the towns.

The Millers' first seventeen months in China had ranged from harsh nightmare to visions of brilliant horizons. The young missionaries had lived and worked under strange and forbidding circumstances, often lower, dingier, and more dangerous than many persons know exist. Committing themselves to Christian discipleship, they had made their way from the "heaven" of America to the Manchu beggars' dens of China. Then, just as they were beginning to realize their hopes, Maude Miller was stricken.

Turning her cooking and household chores over to a helper, she insisted on meeting her dispensary appointments, but finally she became so weak from diarrhea that she could not stand. Even from her bed, her own mouth bleeding and her body wasted, Maude ministered to the waiting Chinese outpatients while her husband was away on an extended trip. Finally, the ravages of a mysterious disease overwhelmed the resistance and courage of the gallant missionary bride, and on March 14, 1905, at the age of twenty-five, Maude Miller passed away.

Exhausted from his recent trip, Harry walked like an aged man as he and his friends Arthur and Bertha Selmon trudged behind the pine-box coffin, pigtails and grief-stricken white faces providing a singularly moving picture, while the compound's Chinese helpers carried Maude to her grave. The white flame of her tragically brief but intensely dedicated life had burned itself out.

IX

PIGTAIL HONEYMOON

THE MOMENTUM of the past two years, an abiding sense of responsibility to those he had brought with him, and a growing devotion to the impoverished millions of China carried Harry Miller across a chasm of sheer desolation, utter loneliness, and grief. He knew what Maude would have wanted; he knew what the Lord expected of him. It was no time to leave China. His job was there.

Harry Miller ignored the pleas of his parents to come home. He plunged more completely than ever into his self-assigned mission. The only respite he allowed himself from day to day was the time he spent in prayer by the little mound of dirt. Feeling helpless without Maude, he was nevertheless strengthened, and before many weeks Harry Miller was making new and important plans.

For two years he worked alone at his station, leading what some would call a splintered life: doctor, printer, teacher, cook, administrator, builder, editor, author, businessman, researcher, and servant to all. But gracefully a Divine Hand seemed to reach down and fuse all those diverse aspects into one China Doctor. Like a tiny cork on a vast sea he bobbed here and there as his ministry ranged over the strange spectrum that was China. But unlike a cork, he absorbed much of that sea and soon became all but immersed in it.

Miller realized that in order to give meaning to the subject matter of the publications he was printing, it was important to relate it insofar as possible to Chinese background. Occasionally, with a helper, he would venture into the hinterland. One trip took him several hundred miles by train and seventy miles by foot to Kaifeng, capital of Honan Province, where he found the remains of a Jewish colony which had come from the Middle East many centuries before. The doctor was excited at the realization that the Hebrews had pushed that far into Asia. The account of the discovery made excellent reading when connected with the Biblical reference to China (Sinim),* and it helped the Chinese to realize that Christianity was not a Western religion, but had come from the East.

On another journey Harry took along a visitor from Washington, D.C., Professor W. W. Prescott, a former president of Battle Creek College, traveling in the Orient to meet with missionaries stationed there. J. N. Anderson, director of the China Division, asked Miller to take the distinguished guest on a trip to Canton and Hong Kong.

The professor had been warned so many times before leaving America about the terrible oriental diseases that he had developed a mania for sanitation which almost ended in a nervous breakdown. He and Miller were traveling down the Pearl River in a small sampan to visit the United States consulate at Canton. At one end of the little vessel was a hut in which the boatmaster and his family lived. After the trip was well under way, one of the nearly naked children of the boatman came out from the sampan shack. She was covered with puffy, pus-filled spots.

"Whatever is the matter with that child?" the professor asked Miller in obvious fear.

* Isa. 49:12.

"Why, that's smallpox."

"Smallpox! What shall we do?" he cried in panic.

"We'll just have to sit here until we get down the river," Miller told him as sympathetically as he could.

The physician recalls: "After all, there wasn't anything else we could do unless he wanted to jump overboard, and there was considerably more disease in those waters than there was on that child's skin. Disease in the Orient was like heat in Hades. There was no place we could avoid it."

Through the trying years after Maude's death, Miller's colleagues, American and Chinese alike, went out of their way to make his life pleasant and to create distractions from the sorrow that sometimes pressed in. "It seemed as if they kept me busy doing a thousand things," he says. "My patients, including missionaries from all denominations, were more than friendly, whether Anglican, Methodist, Baptist, Presbyterian, Episcopalian, Congregational, Lutheran, Disciples of Christ, Latter-day Saints, Roman Catholic, or any one of a dozen other denominational or interchurch groups such as the China Inland Mission and the Door of Hope. Many times I have heard preachers of the great denominations talk about church union. In those early China days there was, regardless of creed, a unity in adversity which the churches of today will perhaps never know. Theological sophistication had not yet swallowed up the primitive godliness of the Christian gospel."

Two years after Maude's death the work had grown sufficiently to warrant sending another family out to join Miller. It was not easy to recruit qualified missionaries in those days, and the Foreign Mission Board searched America in vain. Finally, they located a young man by the name of Arthur Allum in Australia. His name evoked a good deal of fun because people were always misspelling it "Alum." It was common practice to use alum to clarify the water which came from the yellow, silt-laden China rivers. Allum's fiancée, Eva, enthusiastically agreed to join him in the missionary venture, and in less than two months after they were called, Dr. Miller was meeting them, now a honeymooning couple, in Shanghai. He wondered how they would react to China.

The Allums' honeymoon was considerably more exciting than the tailored vacations usually planned by newlyweds. The first thing they had to do was to change into Chinese costume. It was a moving sight to watch them in their gowns laughing each other to tears, all the while reassessing one another in terms of their completely new environment. Dr. Miller's almost total assimilation by his adopted country was hardly reassuring. Two years alone at the mission station had strengthened his Chinese language and clouded the American idiom. He found himself constantly mixing English with Chinese. It began to dawn on him that he was actually thinking more in Chinese than in his native tongue. This, along with his pigtail, he realized later, must have been a shock to the young couple.

The Allums were a strikingly good-looking couple. He was tall, fair-haired, and blue-eyed. She was considerably smaller, with dark eyes and hair, which fitted well into the Chinese background. But Arthur's light hair was a problem. Before they left Shanghai, while Eva was being fitted with Chinese clothes, Miller took her husband to the China Inland Mission where they finally found a light-haired queue. Then they proceeded to a barber who shaved Arthur's head, except for the tuft to which the queue was fastened. All of this was without Eva Allum's knowledge. When Arthur reached home that evening, his head bald except for the topknot and *mao tze*, and with a queue hanging down his back, his bride of four weeks nearly fainted.

"Arthur, how could you do this to me?" Hers was the horrified reaction of a wronged woman.

Harry Miller took the newlyweds by boat from Shanghai to Shangtsai in Honan Province, and there gave them the quarters he and Maude had once had, moving his own things into a room previously occupied by a Chinese helper. He introduced them to the Chinese ways as rapidly and as systematically as he could.

With some reminiscence of Maude, and anxious to please whoever might come into the compound, Miller had spent the last few weeks before the Allums' arrival canning fruit. Cherries by the bucketful had been pitted by the hired help, and then he had cooked and canned them, fondly anticipating the time when the new lady would make them into cherry pie. Unfortunately, Eva Allum knew little about piemaking.

"I trained to be a secretary, Harry," she confided in her prettiest Australian accent. "I have just never learned how to cook, and I know nothing about fixing food."

Obviously, the first thing to do was to teach her to cook. Arthur joined in the game, and before long Eva was one of the best cooks and finest hostesses in China.

As the men turned the house over more and more to the bride, Arthur Allum took an increasing interest in the dispensary. His first series of patients initiated him into the art of handling opium addicts. Many times they were brought in unconscious. Often they tried to commit suicide. Arthur was given the job of putting a rubber tube down their throats into their stomachs in order to wash out as much opium as possible, or at least to minimize the opium absorption. Miller showed him how to stimulate the patients, doing anything to keep them awake until they could eliminate the poison. For some, it was too late.

Arthur, the thoroughgoing student, was determined to do the best possible job. It was not difficult to work the tube down the throats of the patients, because the Chinese were used to aspirating and sucking down noodles. The principal danger was that they might swallow all of it. Arthur developed a system which prevented the whole tube from going down, and he was delighted with his initial success as a stomach washer.

Harry's parents continued to urge him to come home. Realizing finally that to leave China at that time was out of the question with him, they offered to send over his brother Esta if the doctor could support him after he arrived. Esta had a classmate at Mount Vernon Academy, Orvie Gibson, who also wanted to come. Although Harry was concerned that they were traveling more for adventure than from a sense of mission, his loneliness overcame his caution. He invited Esta and Orvie to come.

Fortunately, the newcomers proved to be avid students of the Chinese language, and the three lived cozily in the little room on the compound. The indigenous foods were very cheap. Five American pennies was an average daily wage for a Chinese, and the Americans lived just as the Chinese did. There was no fuel for heating their room, so they put on more clothes when the weather was cold. Sometimes they were able to buy garments that were fur-lined, which carried them through the severe winters of Honan Province. About the only equipment needed from America was bedding, which they carried whenever they traveled on missions from village to village.

Esta's loyalty was a constant inspiration to Miller. He served faithfully for more than seven years, but he died suddenly at his post in 1913 while Miller was in America—"a loss that is still painful to remember."

One of Miller's helpers was Wang T'ien-i, whose name meant "Lord of Heavenly Righteousness." Wang had a little daughter whose upper lip had wasted away to the edge of her nostrils, exposing all of her front teeth. Miller repaired it as best he could, but complete restoration was impossible, and that fact required a great deal of explanation to Wang, who, in turn, became skillful in explaining to others how some persons got well and others did not. Many patients were afflicted with eye trouble. Whenever cataract cases were favorable for surgery, the doctor removed the cataracts. But every favorable case seemed to create more questions in the minds of those whose relatives could not be healed. The missionaries badly needed somebody like Wang to help explain.

Dr. Miller later wrote: "Our idea of missionary work was to help the people help themselves. We came to learn that the genuine hardships in the mission field were not those of physical discomfort, but the spiritual and psychological problems of getting even the simplest truths across to people who have no background for understanding them. For example, surgery requires cleanliness, and so does its aftercare. Many cases successfully completed in surgery were made vastly complex by the carelessness or unconcern for sanitation of relatives who cared for patients. In the typical oriental hospital, even today, most of the care given the patient is provided by relatives and friends who come into the hospital room, to cook and to live there with him.

"Actually, we had no hospital beds at Shangtsai. We just laid our patients down on straw matting on the ground, fed them as best we could, tried to avoid infections and, especially with the eye cases, did our best to avoid high tensions.

"Unfortunately, we had no polished operating room either. As a matter of fact, in the early days we couldn't even operate inside a building, lest some dirt or straw fall down from the ceiling. Nearly all of our surgery had to be done beneath an open sky. Under these conditions we were well aware that most of the healing was being done by God, not by man. Before surgery, we committed every patient to Him."

As the work grew and the colporteurs demanded more and more literature, Miller realized that the publishing plant would have to move to a more central location for shipping and supplies. There was no time to consider the emotional attachments at Shangtsai and the little chapel built beside Maude's grave. They—Harry, the Allums, Orvie, and Esta—were beginning to experience their first real taste of success as missionaries.

About that time a generous churchman in Wisconsin donated

one thousand dollars for the mission work. It seemed like a million
dollars to the struggling group of workers. With it they purchased
a piece of land near the railway station in Sinyang—the same
Sinyang where the original little band of six Americans, led by
missionary Pilquist, had stayed the first night of their journey
into the interior of China. The site for the printing plant had been
selected only after careful searching, and on it was erected a two-
story stone building. As they watched the Chinese handle the
huge stones and maneuver them into place, the missionaries
thought of the building of Jerusalem, and of the temples of
Egypt, Greece, and Rome. Patiently the workers chipped and
shaped the blocks, and the structure rose. It was a real monument.
Prior to that, all of the work—publishing, medicine, evangelism—
had been financed out of the small salaries they had received,
together with what little they had brought with them from their
home countries.

Moving in America was one thing; making a change in China
was quite another. The move from Shangtsai to Sinyang was a
major undertaking. Few Chinese had the slightest appreciation of
the cost and effort it had taken to bring the equipment there. The
loss of one key tool or part could cripple the entire enterprise.
It was necessary to pack and label the equipment with the utmost
care and system.

Sinyang was so crowded that the missionaries could not find a
room to live in while the new buildings were being constructed.
As a last resort they moved into a row of beggars' dens, little
three-walled mud shanties, open on the fourth side, located below
the railroad station. There they lived—the Allums, Orvie, Esta,
and Harry—without protection from mosquitoes, weather, or
filth, their carefully labeled freight piled about them.

Suddenly one day, while Orvie and Esta were in Shangtsai
taking care of some details, Miller came down with a very high
temperature. Suspecting typhus from the plentiful and dangerous
body lice, he accordingly gave the Allums instructions for caring

for him. Although they nursed him tenderly, Harry lapsed into unconsciousness. They worked frantically with water baths in an effort to reduce his temperature, and in desperation they finally decided to risk sending him to the nearest hospital—if he regained consciousness.

A while later the delirious patient did come to, and asked for some quinine, which was used in those days instead of aspirin to reduce temperature. Arthur gave him twenty grains. Five would have been an ample dose. Wrapping him up, the Allums put him in an old wheelchair which had been sent from America earlier, and took him to the train for the trip to the hospital. Arthur accompanied Harry on the miserable journey, leaving Eva to guard the dens alone, lest he return to find everything gone.

After traveling a little way the terrible headache, backache, and miserable feeling began to ease, and Harry began perspiring profusely. The quinine had done its work. He started to sit up when Arthur saw him.

"Get back down there before you kill yourself," Arthur warned. "You are a sick man."

"No, I'm feeling a lot better," Harry insisted. And he was.

The next thing Harry knew, Arthur himself was pulling his clothes tightly around him, shivering, teeth chattering. Harry leaned over and felt Arthur's forehead. He was feverish. By the time they reached Hankow their roles were reversed and Harry had to carry Arthur off the train. The moment they arrived Harry headed for a Chinese apothecary shop for more quinine, and in a short time Arthur was well. Both of them had been victims of malaria.

Meanwhile, they became concerned about Eva. They rushed back to Sinyang as soon as possible to find her huddled, feverish, and half conscious in a corner of one of the dens. Once again the quinine did its work.

It was during the construction of the publishing plant at Sinyang that the J. J. Westrups, a missionary family from Shangtsai, heard of Miller's experience in eye surgery. They met Miller for the first time in the crude dens, but the surgeon's embarrassment, if any, was mitigated by his concern for Mrs. Westrup's eyes which were so badly crossed it was a wonder she could see at all.

"We have come to ask you to operate on my wife's eyes," Westrup informed Harry Miller. Although the doctor could see little expression in Mrs. Westrup's eyes, he sensed her feeling of desperation. Nevertheless, he objected.

"You can see where we are living," Miller pleaded. "All of my instruments are packed somewhere in that pile of boxes." He motioned toward a motley assortment of packing cases, including paper, type, and press equipment as well as medical supplies.

"But we have prayed about this, and we are certain it is the Lord's will," the Westrups insisted. Dr. Miller had heard similar statements about the will of God before, and he was much less certain that it had been properly understood.

"As a matter of fact we have cast lots, and each time the Lord has indicated that you should operate," the couple explained.

Looking at the huts, Miller knew he could not operate in them. "Under these circumstances," he said, "the risk of infection is just too great." He knew by experience that Westerners usually expected much more than the Chinese.

"But, Dr. Miller, you are a Christian surgeon, and you must not doubt the leadings of the Lord," Mrs. Westrup said in anguished tones.

There was nothing to do but make the best of the situation. With coolies assisting them, the Allums sorted out the boxes until they found those marked "instruments." Meanwhile, Esta and Orvie collected together the few sheets they had, and, using bamboo poles for a frame, constructed a temporary tent in the open air. Harry sterilized the instruments in a tiny pan of water over a charcoal fire, and also some silk for the sutures. Finally, Arthur secured more water and boiled some novocain with which to anesthetize Mrs. Westrup's eyes.

With Westrup and their young son, Joseph, standing by to keep away the mosquitoes and the lizards, with Eva running the errands and Arthur assisting in the surgery, Miller performed the operation. Amazingly and providentially, it turned out as successfully as Mrs. Westrup had predicted. Some skeptics might question their conclusions, but to Miller and the Allums it was a constant source of inspiration to see nearly hopeless circumstances turned into God's opportunities.

In the early China days, Dr. Miller was constantly frustrated by the fear of water on the part of the Chinese. They were certain it would give them pneumonia and other diseases and that they would die if they ever bathed. Yet, patients without number came with large ulcers on their legs, and Miller's treatment called for baths of hot and cold wa r to cleanse and to stimulate the circulation in the limbs. He then covered the ulcers loosely with clean bandages. The Chinese usually went to a "medicine shop" where the "doctor" would seal the ulcer with a big plaster, penning up the pus and other secretions, thereby increasing the area of necrosis until the tissue would break down into even larger and more terrible sores.

Finally, Dr. Miller resorted to a device as elementary as the American physician's sugar pills. He put potassium permanganate in the hot water to color it red, and methylene blue in the cold water. The Chinese willingly used the "red medicine" and the "blue medicine." The treatment became famous over the countryside, and so many patients flocked into the room that the staff called it the "ulcerarium." Such simple devices and the help of heaven effected many cures and won doubting hearts.

X

WIFE HUNT

THE HAVOC that can be wrought by well-meaning friends and relatives in a matchmaking mood is unbelievable. Usually conceived of as a humorous situation, one must experience it to know how painful and complex it can be. Inevitably each friend has found "the only one," and to disregard such well-intentioned service is ingratitude of the grossest sort. Throughout the better part of a year—in 1907 and 1908—this was Harry Miller's lot. "Between my parents, the Foreign Mission Board, and intensely interested friends," he recalls, "they had contrived and connived until all arrangements were made for my furlough to America. The trip's unannounced but undenied purpose was to find me a wife."

Those were unfriendly days in which to be traveling. The Russians were fighting the Japanese in Manchuria. The Boxer Rebellion was still recent enough to make a traveler jittery. The opium trade was in its heyday, and nearly everyone was under suspicion as a smuggler. What was to the loved ones at home great anticipation, was to Harry Miller unwelcome realization.

First, he let his hair grow, lest he appear a monstrosity in the Western world. He was a strange-looking "Chinese" indeed, with that hair sticking out from under his *mao tze*. Then came the painful moment when he had to part with the precious queue, which during four years of patient waiting on his part had grown to his waist.

Most difficult of all for Harry was leaving the beloved colleagues he had been responsible for recruiting. But the day came to say goodbye, each going his separate way—the Allums off on a new evangelistic mission, Esta to another station, and Orvie Gibson to still another. The printing work, newly established at Sinyang, would have to remain at a standstill until Harry's return.

The homeward-bound doctor headed for Europe and America by way of Siberia and St. Petersburg, the Russian capital, a journey of five or six thousand miles by land. He was determined to take the shortest ocean crossing possible—anything to avoid the wide Pacific. The trip took him through Manchuria, the garden spot of China, on whose rich soil and minerals the covetous eye of Japan had for some time been focused. The drama of history was truly in the making, and Manchuria was the stage.

Russia was pushing east and south. In 1898, she leased from China the southern part of Liaotung peninsula, which included Talien (renamed Dairen when it passed into Japanese hands at the close of the Russo-Japanese War). She occupied Manchuria at the time of the Boxer Rebellion, and her subsequent failure to depart aroused the fears of Japan, who also had designs on northern China, to the extent that war against Russia was declared in 1904. Few people knew exactly what was happening, for communications were poor in those days, but everyone expected Japan to be wiped off the Chinese map by the great Russian Bear.

However, Japan was successful at every turn. She marched her army across the Yalu River, bordering Korea, into Antung, and down the Liaotung peninsula where she besieged Port Arthur. It seemed certain that she would be stopped at the heavily fortified Russian posts in southern Manchuria. But not so. The Japanese climbed over the bodies of their own comrades, decisively defeated the Russians at Mukden, and went on to command the rest of southern Manchuria before continuing northward.

At this point Russia sent its big fleet to cut off the Japanese supply line. Again the Japanese, brilliant in their own arena of war, cleverly outmaneuvered the powerful Russian fleet and either sank or captured every major Russian ship. Although the war ended officially in 1905 with the signing of the Treaty of Portsmouth, sporadic fighting continued.

When Harry was first being urged by his parents to return to America, some two years before he actually did return, he had discussed the war situation with the American consul general. The fighting, it appeared, was fraught with those strangely humorous overtones which often surround tragedy.

The consul general had explained to Miller in confidence: "Kuropatkin, the commander in chief of the Russian forces in Manchuria, has been gradually falling back and withdrawing. The Czar has been sending him urgent messages inquiring about the progress of the war, but each time Kuropatkin tells him that he is just leading the Japanese on. By now they have 'led the Japs on' a long way toward Siberia. As a matter of fact, the Japanese have taken Tieh Liang, one of the strongest Russian forts on the Manchuria railway.

"Last month the Czar sent word again like this: 'My dear Kuropatkin, please inform me as to the situation of the war. What is the true outlook?' Kuropatkin hastily sent him the answer, 'As I told you before, Honorable Czar, we are just leading the Japanese on.' Finally the Czar in great desperation sent word to the general, 'I pray you, my dear Kuropatkin, please do not lead them on to St. Petersburg.'"

When, at last, Harry did decide to return to America, he set about replenishing his wardrobe. His old shoes had to be replaced. His shirts had shrunk so that the cuffs were halfway to his elbows. After days of bargaining he acquired the semblance of a suit within reach of his pocketbook and, with his meager baggage, set off on the trip.

En route to Russia's Trans-Siberian Railway, Harry Miller looked out upon a China even more desolate than he had known before. During the transfer at Mukden, he sought out the Chinese in a local hotel. Almost before he spoke, they pointed to a little sign hanging in the hotel: DO NOT DISCUSS POLITICAL SITUATIONS OR GOVERNMENTS. The Chinese were especially guarded when discussing events with a foreigner.

Approaching a Chinese hotelkeeper, Miller asked him how Manchuria with the Japanese differed from Manchuria with the Russians.

"Well," replied the hotel man with great care, "when the Russians were here, they employed Chinese to do their errands. The Japanese have come in great numbers, far more than the Russians, and their women work as much as their men. Besides this, they do things the way the Chinese do, and are so used to it that they don't bother hiring the Chinese."

"Is that the only difference?" Miller asked.

"No, there are other things."

The doctor could see that the man was afraid to talk, so he asked him to answer "Chinese style," in a sort of parable.

"You know the Japanese make little biscuits," the hotelkeeper responded, "but the Russians make great big loaves of bread. The Japanese are little people. The Russians are very big men." Without reference to nationalities, he concluded, "Little people have little hearts. Big people have big hearts."

Whether right or wrong, that was the way the Chinese felt, and unfortunately that is the way many of them still feel even though Japan has vastly changed; for the memories of Manchuria live on.

At the Siberian border, Miller had to change from the Japanese-controlled South Manchuria Railway to the Russian-operated Trans-Siberian line. He was reminded of the Chinese hotelkeeper

Harry Willis Miller, M.D., at eighty-one, shortly before his return to the Far East to add a new chapter to his fifty-eight-year career of service.

Harry and Maude Miller adopted Chinese dress soon after their arrival in China in 1903; his cap is a *mao tze*, worn with a queue. Maude's tragic death two years later—caused by sprue, a vitamin-deficiency disease—gave added personal meaning to Miller's later nutritional research.

At a meeting of missionaries held in Shanghai in 1907, shortly before his first furlough to America, Harry Miller bade temporary farewell to many of his friends in China. Miller, who had already sacrificed his queue in favor of a Western haircut, stands at the right in the group of three bearded men (back row). On the left in the same row is W. W. Prescott, onetime president of Battle Creek College. In front of Miller, wearing Chinese dress, are Arthur and Eva Allum. Third and fourth from the left in the same row are Bertha and Arthur Selmon with a Chinese baby whom they had adopted. Seated second and third from the left in the next row are the J. J. Westrups. Mrs. Westrup had earlier undergone eye surgery performed by Dr. Miller. Seated in the center of the same row, holding a baby, is J. N. Anderson, China pioneer missionary, with Mrs. Anderson to his left. To her left are Erik Pilquist—who had taken Miller to Hsintsai upon his arrival in China in 1903—and Mrs. Pilquist, both in Chinese dress.

Harry and Marie Iverson Miller at the time of their marriage in 1908. A trained nurse, she served with him through forty-two years of missionary activity, and reared their four children.

Shanghai Sanitarium, opened January 1, 1928, the first of fifteen hospitals to be established in China under the leadership of Harry Miller, who also founded numerous smaller clinics.

Members of the Shanghai Sanitarium staff see Harry Miller off, one day in the mid-thirties, for a round of surgery in interior China. Standing to the doctor's right is his wife Marie. When going to outlying places, Dr. Miller had to take with him all necessary medical equipment. He frequently traveled by plane in order to cover his widespread practice.

Harry Miller and Marshal Chang Hsüeh-liang at Hankow airport in 1935, two years after Dr. Miller had cured the Young Marshal's opium addiction. In the background is the Young Marshal's Boeing transport plane which was frequently placed at the doctor's disposal.

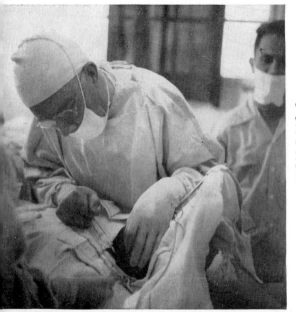

One of the most skilled and experienced surgeons in the world, Harry Miller has carried out more than eighteen thousand operations. Here he performs a thyroidectomy during one of his frequent visits to hospitals in Manila.

Wuhan Sanitarium and Hospital at Wuchang, one of the medical units established through the generosity of the Young Marshal and the scene of Miller's activities as "mayor" in the late thirties. Twenty thousand refugees moved into the Sanitarium compound when Hankow capitulated to the Japanese in 1938.

Two mission aides view the ruins of the Wuchang city dispensary, destroyed by Japanese bombs in 1938. From under this rubble, Dr. Miller rescued a clinic worker and a baby.

Dr. Miller examines a soybean plant grown on his farm in Mount Vernon, Ohio.

Harry Miller demonstrates his small-scale soy-milk processing machine, which can be operated by one person. The goal of Japan's Ministry of Health is to install one of these in each of the thirty thousand village *tofu* (soy cheese) factories in Japan.

Japan this youngster lives on Soyalac, one of the products made possible through Dr. Miller's research. The child could take neither breast milk nor animal milk without becoming covered from head to toe with atopic eczema.

Soy-milk booths like this one are common on the streets of Hong Kong, where more Soyalac is sold than any kind of soft drink.

One of Dr. Miller's patients at the Benghazi, Libya, hospital in 1956 was little Mohammed Ali, a Bedouin child, suffering from malnutrition bordering on starvation. When he was brought in from his desert home, he was too weak to cry. Under Dr. Miller's expert care, Ali grew strong and healthy and began to take a lively interest in the world around him. The word spread rapidly, and soon dozens of persons from the desert tribes were bringing their ailing children to the doctor's door.

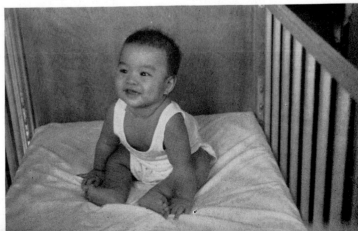

Generalissimo Chiang Kai-shek greets Mrs. Mary Greer Miller while Madame Chiang congratulates Dr. Miller following ceremonies held March 26, 1956, in which Miller received the Blue Star of China, that country's highest award, similar to the Congressional Medal of Honor of the United States.

at Mukden as he noted the difference between the trains. The
Japanese used tiny cars on a gauge much narrower than that of
American railroads, and little engines which bounced along like
a Toonerville Trolley. The Russian trains were giants in com-
parison, the tall, broad coaches running on tracks even wider than
those in America.

Miller was given a compartment with a Russian student who
glued himself to the doctor, going with him every place, even
to the station washroom. But he was of little help because he
could speak neither English nor Chinese. Venturing into the
dining car, Miller found that the menu was in Russian. His attempts at sign language were useless, whereupon the waiter
brought a French menu. From Miller's point of view, it might as
well have been in Arabic or Sanskrit. Finally, an obliging traveler
across the aisle ordered a dinner for him, which turned out to be
anything but a vegetarian's delight, for Harry had been a vegetarian from his Battle Creek days onward. It was the only time
on the six-day trip that he went into the dining room, choosing,
rather, to buy his food from vendors during station stops.

When he met some American friends at St. Petersburg, Harry
Miller discovered to his chagrin that less than five years with the
Chinese had cost him fluency in his mother tongue—a strange experience known to many persons residing in foreign countries.
Wherever he met English-speaking travelers—in St. Petersburg,
Helsingfors, Stockholm, Copenhagen, Hamburg—he struggled to
relate clearly the story of China missions. Except for a second
attack of malaria, he found himself enjoying the relief which
the beautiful European cities afforded him from the desperate
misery and filth of China, although he felt almost disloyal to his
adopted land.

Despite his trouble with the English language, Harry was able
in London to acquire that which he needed very badly. In the
few days he was there, London haberdashers turned him out after
the manner of a king. Never again was he dressed so well. After

his shopping spree and some six weeks since his departure from China, he boarded ship for North America. Several uneventful days out of Liverpool found the vessel in the still waters of the St. Lawrence, a few hours from the Millers' home at St. John, New Brunswick, Canada.

Harry's father had become a minister and was at that time president of the Maritime Conference (New Brunswick) of the Seventh-day Adventist Church. Harry divided his time between visits with his parents and Church work in the United States. "Being in America again gave me a strange feeling," he says. "Many emotions disturbed me as I went from place to place. It was surprising what little things would stir up memories—train whistles, American carriages, and glistening white church steeples. I came to realize that few Americans recognized them for what they were—monuments to a glorious heritage."

There was little time for relaxation, however. His father and mother reminded him that many plans had been made for his furlough, and it was soon evident that these would involve women at every turn. Matters eventually reached the point where Harry was afraid to speak to any unmarried woman, no matter how attractive, for fear she might think he had plans for her.

George Irvine, president of the General Conference of the Seventh-day Adventist Church, brought Harry some relief with a series of camp-meeting tours, which gave him an opportunity to speak of his heart's first concern—the needs of China. He became so involved in soliciting funds that there was seldom time to think about a possible wife, except, of course, when an ever thoughtful friend came along with another prospect. Even if Harry had become interested, the ten-day camp meetings were hardly long enough to make an assessment that would justify a proposal of marriage.

Miller reminded his friends that anyone who might think of marrying him had to consider not only a man but a doctor. More than that, he was a missionary bent on returning to a difficult field; China was a long, long way from America in those days.

The whole summer passed, and Harry was no nearer to selecting a bride. "I could see that the General Conference officials were beginning to get the jitters," he says. "The normal service period between furloughs was seven years and I had been gone only four, so my furlough was to be short."

William A. Spicer, secretary of the General Conference, asked Harry one day if he were ready to go back.

"Yes, certainly," said Miller.

"Well, we're not going to send you back alone," he told the young doctor kindly but firmly.

"Not even if I want to?" he asked.

"Not a chance," Spicer replied. "Besides, there are plenty of young women, thoroughly eligible."

"Well," Harry answered, "if there are, I haven't been able to find them, and I suppose I am the one to do the choosing."

It wasn't that he was so terribly particular, he later insisted, but he knew the problems that lay ahead, and certain of his well-wishing friends simply were not facing them. About that time an idea flashed into Spicer's mind.

"I think it would be a good plan for you to give a series of lectures at the Foreign Mission Seminary," Spicer told Harry one day. He said no more about marriage, but it was not hard for Miller to judge his motives. Harry fell into the plot somewhat skeptically but not unwillingly. His loneliness had been very real since Maude's death.

The Foreign Mission Seminary was located in Maryland, just over the line from Washington, D.C., and directly across from it stood the school of nursing operated by the Church's Washington Sanitarium. Before long, Harry was dividing his time between lectures at the seminary and teaching at the school of nursing.

One day Mrs. Irvine, wife of the General Conference president and formerly Harry's matron at Mount Vernon Academy, came to see the young missionary. She was then Sanitarium matron, and also held a position at the nursing school. It suddenly occurred to Harry that she was well-qualified to be the "middle woman." And why not, he reasoned. In China, no marriage was completed without a middle man, and he had become more Chinese than American.

Dr. Miller still remembers those teaching days at the school of nursing. "As the weeks passed, I began to notice more and more an engaging miss who usually sat near the back of the room, as if forewarned of my intentions. After several weeks I decided that she was the one. The question was, would she want me? Anyone who married me would have to marry China, too."

The girl was Marie Iverson, from Maine. She had enrolled at the school of nursing because her widowed aunt, Bothilde Miller, was a head nurse there. Marie was living with her. Some time later, after lengthy discussions with Mrs. Irvine and Aunt Bothilde, Marie promised to marry the young China Doctor. But there was one stipulation.

"However, I will be very pleased if Aunt Bothilde may go with us," Marie added, looking primly up into her suitor's eyes.

"Aunt Bothilde to China!" Harry exclaimed, startled.

This was an unexpected development. At least, he reasoned, Aunt Bothilde had a distraction of her own—Percy, an adopted boy, seven years old.

"Does she *really* want to go?" he asked.

"Yes, she would like to be a missionary, too." Marie's interest now almost bordered on enthusiasm.

They presented the proposition to the General Conference officers, and the plan was approved, although Dr. Daniel H. Kress, the Sanitarium's medical director, was not happy at the prospect of losing three good workers.

Harry's father performed a simple wedding ceremony in Marie's home in Portland, Maine, and soon the newlyweds were off across the United States to the Pacific Coast and China. At Seattle, they boarded a ship for the dreaded trans-Pacific trip. Many passengers became sick, and as usual, Harry was the sickest of all. He was relieved when they arrived in Yokohama, and unspeakably happy when they landed at Shanghai.

Harry's happiness dimmed a little when he found that he was to remain in Shanghai. He had learned to love Central China, and after his trip through the north to Siberia, he had realized all the more the needs of China's interior. But the Church leaders felt rightly that the center of the work should be near a metropolis, and Shanghai with its port and railroads was the most suitable place. Already, the printing press had been shipped there.

After much searching, the Millers located a house on the north side, and there the family settled down—Harry, Marie, Aunt Bothilde, and little Percy. Before long they were joined by Bert Roberts and his wife from California's Pacific Press Publishing Association. With Roberts' ability as a printer and Mrs. Roberts' competence as a proofreader, Miller was freed for nearly full-time medical and editorial work.

They were fortunate in finding a building to house their printing establishment. Its owner was Charlie Soong, father of three daughters and three sons, all destined for outstanding careers. Charlie Soong, who had been educated in America, spoke good English and was both generous and witty. He had a printing plant of his own, but his building was larger than he required.

"We certainly appreciate your renting us part of this building," Miller told him gratefully after completing their agreement.

"That is good," Soong answered, "but I will have to put up a partition between your men and mine."

"Oh, no, you don't need to go to all that expense," Harry assured him. "We can keep on our own side."

"When two companies use the same building," the older man volunteered, sagely, "there are apt to be some misunderstandings. There, of course, will never be any trouble between you and me. But," he added, eyes twinkling, "we have no control over the feelings of our workmen. You remember Abraham and Lot. They

got along fine, but their servants didn't. So they had to part." He
bowed Dr. Miller out of the room—and soon put up the partition.

As time passed, Harry and Marie Miller and their colleagues
came to see more and more the hand of God in those early negotia-
tions with Charlie Soong. For in the years that followed, Charlie's
daughters became three of China's greatest women: Madame H.
H. Kung, Madame Sun Yat-sen, and Madame Chiang Kai-shek. In
part through this business association and the friendship growing
from it, Harry Miller was destined to become one of China's best-
known doctors, personal physician to the Chiang Kai-sheks and
surgeon to Madame Sun Yat-sen—families now parted by the
Bamboo Curtain.

XI

SOME CLOSE CALLS

"THERE'S A MAN——there's a man trying to get into my room!"

The shrill voice shattering the stillness of the night was Aunt Bothilde's. She had run up the stairs from her rooms to the Millers' apartment with a speed out of all proportion to her weight and age. Harry, who was already in bed, hurriedly threw on a kimono while Auntie continued her frightened sputterings.

"He's down there pounding on the window, asking to come in!"

"You stay here with Marie," Harry admonished, as, barefooted, he headed for the street. Sure enough, there the culprit was, still rapping on the window.

"What *are* you doing here?" Harry demanded.

"That is none of your business," the stranger answered curtly in the language of a cultured Chinese.

"But it *is* my business. This is my home, and we are not used to being disturbed at this time of night," Harry answered sharply.

The Chinese made a move as if to push aside his inquisitor, and Harry's temper suddenly boiled over. It seemed ridiculous later, but in a moment he had the Chinese down flat, overcoat and all, and was sitting on his victim's chest, his bare feet on the young fellow's arms, his hands against the man's chin. The frightened Chinese pleaded for Harry to let him go.

"Not until I turn you over to the police," replied Harry in a determined tone.

Suddenly the prowler's brother appeared, extremely agitated, to plead for his release. Harry felt, however, that it was a matter for the police; he hesitated to take a chance when the safety of his family was concerned . . .

Early the next morning the brother reappeared, begging Harry to secure the release of the fellow from police custody.

"My brother, you know, is a teller in the Shanghai and Hong Kong Bank. We two boys have an aged mother who is very dependent upon us. Surely you will not require him to be publicly tried. He will lose his job and be thrown into prison! It is just that he likes the American lady very much. He wouldn't hurt anybody."

By that time Harry's temper had cooled—and he had learned the rest of the story. Aunt Bothilde, who was an active missionary —selling literature, visiting homes, teaching Bible classes—was diligently trying to master the Chinese language. In the process, she had attracted the attention of the young Chinese, who had fallen in love with her, although she was unaware of his feelings. So, after extracting a promise from the brother that the man would not bother Auntie in the future, Harry asked the police to release him.

Auntie's desperate suitor never came again.

After that, life moved along smoothly for some time. Relieved of his printing duties, Miller made progress with his dispensary and his editorial work. Soon Arthur Selmon, working in a country clinic, was invited to come and take over the editorial function in order to free Miller for general leadership responsibilities within the mission's China Division. The missionaries were proud of their new press room which, under Bert Roberts' direction, had become nearly as systematic and up-to-date as a shop in America. Then, one night, Miller was roused from sleep.

"*Fung chung!* Fire! Fire!" frantic voices were screaming. "The press is on fire!" Impossible, Harry thought, as he leaped from his bed. They must have the wrong place. But, racing down the road, he saw that it was indeed true. "Everything was going up in smoke," says Miller, "our presses, our type, our cutters, and all of the tediously made cases, melted or burned to the ground." At the moment he arrived, some of the helpers, with amazing courage, were throwing books out of the upstairs window of the blazing building. Those books were all that was saved.

It was some time before the press could be re-established.

In quest of a retreat away from the summer humidity of Shanghai and the Yangtze valley, the mission had purchased at a very low price a resort at Mokanshan Mountain in the Ou Hills near Hangchow. Marie and Harry moved there, and he commuted to Shanghai. In November of 1908, Marie returned to the city for the birth of their first child, Maude May. In the filth of crowded Shanghai, one of the most disease-ridden cities of the world, bearing a child was a real hazard.

Four months after Maude's birth, Marie became very ill. In an effort to save her life, Harry rented a Chinese houseboat to take her to the hill resort at Mokanshan. With two boatmen pushing in the rear with poles, and two pulling from the front as they walked along the shore, the boat moved slowly up the shallow Yangtze, every minute an hour.

Little Maude, accustomed to breast feeding, cried for food, and no one knew what to do with the hungry baby of a sick American mother. There were no prepared foods then. As was their custom, Marie and Harry took the problem to God, and rejoiced at His prompt answer. A Chinese woman, the wife of one of the boatmen, had given birth a month or so before, and was nursing her child. She offered to nurse the American baby, too.

That generous mother was taught as much about sanitation in a few hours as the average woman learns in a lifetime. At first, Marie did not know what to think, but as far as little Maude was concerned, it made no difference whether it was American or

Chinese milk, just so her tummy was full. The trip was finished in peace.

Relieved of care and concern for her little one, Marie made an astonishing recovery and was soon able to care for her baby herself. Before the year was out, the mission family was joined at the Hills Station by Dr. August Larson, and together they set up their first real medical unit in China. It was at the same station that the Millers' second daughter, Ethel Marie, was born in 1910. Except for Ethel's attack of polio shortly after her birth, the girls grew without event, to become a strong help to their parents.

In the winter of 1908-1909, when J. N. Anderson returned to General Conference headquarters in America, Miller was assigned as leader of the Church's general mission in China. Within a year the work began to take on new momentum, and Miller's medical practice suffered from neglect. To ease the situation, the General Conference agreed to send a full-time superintendent for the China field, which released Miller to return to his beloved Central China to strengthen the medical work there and to start a school. With Marie and their two little ones, he traveled overland, first by railway and then by two-wheeled horsecart, to Chouchiakou. Accommodations for missionaries in Honan Province had been somewhat improved by then. There was even the luxury of a wooden floor in the Chouchiakou house, and in that building was started the Church's first school in China, which was later to become the well-known China Training Institute located near Nanking.

The missionaries gave their first students unusual attention, even hiring a houseboat to take them to the school. Dr. Miller made the trip up the river, and it was memorable. At one point it was decided to pull along the shore for church services. Worship was interrupted by the violent quarreling of the boatman and his wife, who could be heard well above the hymns. The worshipers did not know what all the trouble was about, and it was not their place to interfere in a family quarrel. From the wife's gasps, yells, and screaming, it sounded almost as though she were being killed.

Later, as the boat started upstream again, the husband discovered that the rear end of the boat was sliding over toward the bank. He started for the cabin, shouting to his wife to get to the rudder, but there was no response. Again and again he yelled, but still no reply. Finally, he looked down through the hole in the roof of the cabin where their sleeping child lay on the bunk. Nearby, his wife hung by a rope—a common method of suicide in China.

"*Mai dai fu, Mai dai fu!* Dr. Miller, Dr. Miller!" rang out in horrified tones.

People appeared from all quarters, but none of them dared to touch the poor woman. They drew back in fear, making way for the doctor as he approached. Miller lowered himself into the cabin and cut the rope from the woman's neck. Limp and with no perceptible breathing, she was apparently dead. But the doctor listened closely and thought he detected a faint heartbeat. Quickly he brought her up to the deck where he gave her artificial respiration until she began to breathe normally.

No more quarreling was heard for the rest of that journey.

XII

A KEY DECISION

SOME MONTHS after the inauguration of the school program in Honan Province, Dr. Miller was stricken again, as he had been on previous occasions, with the mysterious illness which had taken Maude's life. Its diarrhea, enteritis, and inflammation of the small intestine along with atrophy of the liver and ulceration of the mouth brought its victims down with severe discomfort, frequently with agony. In the grip of the disease, Miller became more and more emaciated, and he could retain little food. His recovery was only partial, and very gradual.

In the spring of 1911 the Millers were called to a mission meeting in Shanghai. Harry was still so far from well, and the children so small, that they had to hire a mulecart to take them to the nearest railway station, forty miles distant, where they hoped to get a train for Hankow, the point at which they would board the river steamer for Shanghai. During the first part of the journey, the Millers slept with the mules at night in whatever shelter was available. They covered the dirt floor with straw and cornstalks for a bed, placing Maude and Ethel between them so that the restless mules would not hurt the children.

At Shanghai the leaders were quick to note Miller's rapidly failing health, and they decided that if he were to be saved for

China he would have to return to America at once. The entire mission company joined in earnest prayer that the doctor be spared to receive the medical attention America could provide.

That trip was a sad sequel to the couple's ambitions. Harry's pain was compounded by his concern for Marie and their two baby girls, cooped up with him in the ship's hold. He kept wondering if he would ever again see China and all the faithful workers left behind.* Many times he had been through the corridors of death with others. He knew those shadows well, and he was almost convinced that this was his time.

At the San Francisco customs office, just untying their few belongings was a major task for the weary pair, but the officers were taking no chances on opium smugglers in those days. Seventy-five miles away, overlooking Robert Louis Stevenson's Silverado Trail near the head of famed Napa Valley, the Church operated St. Helena Sanitarium. The kindly San Francisco station agent who sold the Millers rail tickets carried the two little girls, one in each arm, as Marie helped Harry stagger to his seat on the train that took them to the Sanitarium.

Marie and the children stayed with Harry at the Sanitarium for a few days before leaving for her parents' home in Portland, Maine, three thousand miles away. Harry moved from hospital to hospital searching for a cure, but the cause of his disease was not then known. The newly formed American Society of Tropical Medicine took time from a New Orleans meeting to study his symptoms. When all agreed that his case was hopeless, Harry Miller simply decided he would not die. He headed for his parents' home in New Brunswick, where Marie and the children joined him. Soon he began to realize that he was at least holding his own; he stopped losing weight, and before long it occurred to him that he was beginning to enjoy his food.

Subsequent medical research has revealed that this disease—now

---

* Among those left behind were Aunt Bothilde and Percy. Later, the boy was sent back to America to a boarding school but Aunt Bothilde stayed on in China, although she, too, returned to the United States eventually.

called sprue—is, like pellagra, caused by vitamin deficiencies. It is readily corrected today by the particular use of folic acid and B vitamins. Choosing to go directly to his home was a decision that saved Harry's life. There he ate heartily of fresh vegetables and fruits, and within a matter of weeks he was strong enough to secure a part-time job shingling houses in New Brunswick for a dollar a day. That good food gave him his start. Rest, and activity in the fresh air, completed the cure.

Uncle Ben Honeyman, husband of the Aunt Catherine who had loaned Harry money in his medical-school days and himself a wealthy farmer, had been from the first violently opposed to Harry's China mission. "If I have a whole pot of gold coins," he had once told Harry angrily, "you will never get one of them if you ever go to China." But now Uncle Ben, an old man, sent word from his western-Ohio home that he would like to see his nephew. When the Millers arrived there they found him in torture from a fractured hip, suffered in a fall three days earlier. He had had no medical care at all; doctors were not readily available, and the Honeymans probably would not have bothered with one anyway.

He and his wife, unaware of the extent of the injury, had tried to immobilize his leg, to prevent excruciating pain and in the empty hope that he would soon recover. He was in misery—a wealthy man, owner of several farms and one of the richest persons in the county, lying on an old cot with filthy, worn garments packed around him. There was a stench from the odor of soiled clothing which had not been changed since the accident.

Harry had planned only a brief visit, but when he saw the situation he realized it demanded his attention. First, he bought a hospital bed for Uncle Ben. Then, mustering what strength he could, Harry cleaned up the old man's room. It was stacked full of auction "finds" that Aunt Catherine had picked up here and there. Looking for bargains had become a mania, and she bought and stored items, regardless of their needs, until their home was literally a storeroom for useless objects. When the patient grew stronger, Harry procured a wheelchair. Uncle Ben's appreciation was touching.

One day Aunt Catherine called Harry aside and asked him about his plans for the future.

"I think we will settle in Mount Vernon, Ohio, where I will practice for a while until we are out of debt, and then we plan to return to China," he replied.

Aunt Catherine said nothing, but went to Uncle Ben's room, returning a few minutes later to ask Harry how much he would charge to stay and take care of them.

"It isn't a question of charging," he told her. "It's just a matter of necessity to make three thousand dollars in the next year. I can easily do that in practice."

"My, three thousand dollars is an awful price," she moaned, apparently oblivious of his explanations. "To think how we have scrimped and saved through the years . . ."

And saved they had. Aunt Catherine was still milking their cows and raising their own chickens although she and her husband were worth a quarter of a million dollars. But in Uncle Ben's mind there was no question. Harry's care was the first real attention he had ever received, and it was well worth three thousand dollars. So, even though Harry had already obtained his Ohio state medical license, he changed his plans and stayed on.

Seventeen weeks later Uncle Ben died.

"I need you more than ever now, Harry," Aunt Catherine said.

Harry made the funeral arrangements, and at almost the same time he had to set up crop schedules. His early experience on the Ohio farm stood him in good stead. Next, he took care of the final details of Uncle Ben's will, which left everything to Aunt Catherine. Then one night, while Marie was putting the girls to bed, Harry and his aunt were sitting by the fire when she asked a hard question.

"Harry," she inquired in her slow way, conscious of the weight of her proposition, "if I make a will leaving all I have to you, would you be willing to stay and take care of our farms and me as long as I live?"

After some thought, Harry agreed. Aunt Catherine called a lawyer and made out her will, leaving everything to her nephew in fee simple. The will was placed in the safe-deposit vault at the bank. For a full year Harry stayed on at the farm, convalescing from sprue and managing his aunt's affairs. As promised, she paid the three thousand dollars, with which he cleared all of his debts; and he still had money left.

After a year of recuperation, Harry's conscience began to bother him. About that time, Professor Ben Wilkinson asked Harry if he would teach Bible at Mount Vernon Academy. The invitation threw him into a turmoil of heart and soul. Here he was, a physician, one who had dedicated his life to foreign missions, managing farms for an aging aunt. He was shocked to realize that he was beginning to love money more than he cared to admit. He and Marie talked things over, and they agreed that their real happiness lay in broader service.

He took a temporary teaching job at Mount Vernon Academy at thirteen dollars a week, not a large wage for a family of five— for in December, 1912, the family had been increased by the arrival of a third child and first son, Harry Willis, Jr. However, they were thankful to be well, and they found the living adequate. But, important as the work was, Harry was convinced that his field of service still lay in surgery and research rather than in teaching.

There remained the touchy question of what to do about Aunt Catherine and the estate. It was solved by bringing in Harry's father for a year. After that, the whole matter was turned over to Harry's brother Clarence. When Aunt Catherine died nearly ten years later, her estate was divided among numerous relatives, but nothing went to Harry. Yet he was far richer, for he had happiness and satisfactions which no money could purchase.

XIII

OPERATING ON THE SIAMESE ELEPHANT

Washington Sanitarium was in trouble. It had been established by the Seventh-day Adventist Church in 1907, and it had never been solvent. Patients were few and debts were many. I. H. Evans, a long-time friend of Harry Miller, was chairman of the Sanitarium board. Remembering Harry's astuteness with finances in China and his medical skill in Chicago and Battle Creek days, Evans decided he must somehow bring Miller to Washington, D.C. His first step was to arrange to have Harry Miller elected medical secretary for the General Conference, a position that entailed world-wide responsibilities. Professor Ben Wilkinson persuaded Harry to accept. It was less than a year before the outbreak of the First World War that the Miller family moved to Maryland, and Harry took up his new duties at the Washington headquarters of the Church.

Shortly after his arrival, Dr. Miller overheard two members of the Washington Sanitarium board talking about "the big Siamese elephant." What, he asked, did they mean?

"See that gray building over there?" Evans pointed to the main Sanitarium building, which stood in Takoma Park, Maryland, just over the Washington, D.C., line. "I would call it a white elephant, except that it is gray, just the color of those 'white' elephants in Siam. It has us one hundred sixty-eight thousand dollars in debt!"

Later, when Harry was sitting on the steps of one of the Foreign Mission Seminary buildings across from the Sanitarium lawn, Francis W. Wilcox, newly elected chairman of the Sanitarium board, came along and sat down beside him.

"Miller," he said with a quiet urgency, "I have important news for you."

"Yes?" Harry queried, sensing impending disaster.

"Our board has voted unanimously to invite you to act as medical superintendent of Washington Sanitarium."

"I already have a job," Harry gasped, "and, besides, I'm not qualified for a hospital superintendency. You know I've been out of this country for nearly ten years, and in medicine you just have to keep ahead."

"But we don't know where else to turn." The chairman seemed desperate.

"I'm telling you it would be folly," Miller insisted.

"Then perhaps you could make a suggestion," was the challenge.

That stumped Harry. His friend Dr. John Harvey Kellogg and several associates were no longer in the active employ of the Church. Medical administrators were scarce. Caught in a dilemma, Harry could only keep muttering that he was too far behind the times.

Wilcox saw his opening.

"We are certain you can handle it, and we will give you every opportunity for refresher courses at a hospital or medical school of your choice," he promised.

About that time Evans strode up, and Miller looked to him for consolation. He looked in vain, for Evans was solidly behind Wilcox. They expressed gratitude to Harry for his dedication to the work of the Church, and finally he could see that there was no escape. A few days later Harry registered at Johns Hopkins

University Hospital in Baltimore for postgraduate study in surgery.

Managing a hospital on the brink of financial ruin, commuting forty rough miles back and forth to Baltimore every day for study, and trying to keep up with his work for the General Conference left Harry with no leisure. Then, to cap it all, an epidemic gripped the Sanitarium and felled a major segment of the staff.

Ptomaine poisoning was the immediate verdict. Dr. Miller, however, believed it to be an infectious disease. Typhoid was his diagnosis, and it had been spread, he believed, by fly contamination of the food. Members of the staff disputed his conclusion, and he had to set about to prove himself right. Meanwhile, the superintendent of nurses died.

Following sterile procedures, Miller had one of the nurses draw blood from six of the patients. He took the specimens to Johns Hopkins bacteriological laboratory, where they were plated and cultured. Five out of the six samples showed pure cultures of typhoid bacillus.

That diagnosis established Harry Miller's reputation with the staff physicians, whose lives he had saved, and it further underscored one of his guiding principles: Never guess if you can help it; look past the symptoms to discover the true nature of the disease before you apply the remedy.

However, the Sanitarium was still far from healthy, financially. There was not enough business at the hospital to enable Miller to keep abreast of medical practices. Later, he often joked that making his rounds involved, principally, shaking hands with three or four old ladies. As a last resort for surgical experience, the doctor actually set up an animal hospital on the back lawn of the Sanitarium.

It was a trying time. Says the doctor: "When one talks about experimenting with the precepts of God, some intellectuals wonder if that person has his head screwed on straight. I have always felt sorry for those cynics, for they are missing one of life's most precious experiences. I would cherish for them my privilege of studying the infinitely complex physiology and co-ordinated anatomy of the human body, which could not conceivably have just happened or evolved. They simply don't understand the marvelous way God works, His wonders to perform. And it was a strange way that God used to place the Sanitarium on its feet."

The "strange way" appeared in the form of a new patient—Benny Walsh by name. Benny, a diminutive hunchbacked elevator operator with a sunny disposition, was well known around the area. He had visited famous surgeons from New York to Virginia to find relief from an ulcer and from internal complications growing out of his doubled-up posture. Now he came to Dr. Miller.

"I am not at all sure I can help you," the surgeon admitted readily. He knew, as had the other surgeons, that operating on Benny entailed great risk.

"But I've been told by many people that you are a surgeon of wide experience and that I can trust myself implicitly to you," the hunchback answered confidently. His assurance was considerably greater than Miller's. There was nothing to do but operate. "If I ever asked for Divine Help over a patient before, I did over the operating table that day," says Dr. Miller. "When a patient stakes his all on you, is utterly helpless in your hands, with his whole future, health, and welfare depending on your skill and judgment, it is a serious matter. Surgeons are far more concerned than many patients think."

Benny's chest leaned forward at nearly a right angle to his hips and legs. Instead of having an abdomen that was in line and parallel with other parts of the body, it lay horizontal when he was standing up, and the abdominal wall pushed up and down as he breathed. Benny could not lie flat on the operating table because of his hunched back. And of course he could not lie on his side for an abdominal incision, so the doctor and nurses propped him up with pillows as best they could, and asked the anesthetist, a woman physician, to administer the anesthetic.

"Tell the patient to lie down," she instructed Dr. Miller.

"But this patient cannot lie down," he replied.

"Dr. Miller, you can easily see that I cannot reach up with the ether cone to give him anesthetic in this sitting position," she insisted.

"Then take the stool here and stand on it," he suggested. "You can adjust. He can't." And with that they went ahead.

Because of the abdominal movement caused by each breath Benny took, Dr. Miller had to adjust his every motion, while cutting the tissues and suturing, to the patient's breathing. Nevertheless, he found the ulcer he had anticipated, and he then did a Finney pyloroplasty after the manner of Dr. John Finney, his postgraduate instructor at Johns Hopkins. Benny's recovery was uneventful.

After that, Benny walked the streets of Takoma Park, Maryland, and Washington, D.C., publishing widely the remarkable change in his health. His face filled out and he made an excellent appearance, a living advertisement for the Sanitarium. Soon patients were pouring in. As word spread to Capitol Hill, congressmen, senators, judges of the Supreme Court, and ambassadors visited the Sanitarium. Miller's services were so valuable that duty required him to remain at the Sanitarium throughout the First World War.

William Jennings Bryan frequently went to Washington Sanitarium over weekends, during the period he served as secretary of state. As a boy, Harry had known of him and had followed his name in the press, never thinking Bryan would one day be his patient and dinner guest. Bryan greatly enjoyed horseback riding and would ride six or eight miles out from the Capitol for the Sanitarium's vegetarian meals, which he greatly enjoyed.

Sometimes Miller tried to draw him out on the question of evolution, and once he mentioned a stalactite he had seen in Luray Caverns in Virginia, which had been broken off some forty years before, and was renewing itself. He repeated the guide's words that considering its volume, length, size, and the rate of the drip of lime water which had built it up, it must have taken over a million years to form. What, asked Miller, did Bryan think of that?

"You, of course, know a baby will about triple its weight during the first year of growth, Dr. Miller," the statesman answered. "If a human being continued at the same ratio of growth every year, you can appreciate the size he would be in a short period of time. There is absolutely no reason to believe that the rate of drip in those caverns today is the same as it was centuries ago."

Alexander Graham Bell was another man who spent some time at the Sanitarium. He had developed the habit of sleeping a good part of the day and of doing most of his work at night when there was least chance of interruption. One time Miller mentioned his own interest in longevity and prolonging the lives of the peoples of the world, and asked Bell if he had any suggestions.

"Dr. Miller," Bell answered with a sparkle in those sharp eyes of his, "I can tell you if you or your friends want to live to a great age, my findings indicate that you should choose ancestors of great length of life."

As consulting physician, Dr. Miller served two presidents—Taft and Wilson—and the wife of another president, Harding. During the First World War, Woodrow Wilson named Miller to Herbert Hoover's American Relief Administration. "I remember in later years," says Miller, "when former premier of China, T'ang Shao-i, asked me to take his greetings to his friend President Hoover. I was told by the president's secretary that I would have four or five minutes.

"When I asked the secretary how I would know when I should leave, he said that the president would arise, which would be the signal. Herbert Hoover had been a consulting engineer in China, and he had many questions. After talking about such China warlords as Wu P'ei-fu, Li Tsung-jen, P'ei Chung-shih, Ho Ying-chin, and others for the better part of an hour, I wondered if the president ever would arise. He didn't. He showed a tremendous interest every moment, and finally with my eye on the nervous secretary in the doorway, I told the president that I thought I had presumed on his time long enough, shook hands with him, and left."

By the early twenties, Washington Sanitarium was well out of debt, and had expanded considerably. Except for meager living expenses, Dr. Miller had turned back into the hospital all of his fees, amounting to upwards of fifty thousand dollars a year. That money supplemented the hospital's charity budget. Yet, as with nearly every prosperous institution, the Sanitarium was a target for unscrupulous "friends." Dr. Miller still remembers them: "Many salesmen tried to sell us things the hospital didn't need." They would urge unnecessarily large inventories of supplies and equipment. The era of high-pressure salesmanship was just coming into vogue. And as any modern hospital manager knows, every small corner has to be watched. Temptation to thievery or waste must be removed as far as possible. Washington Sanitarium was not without its share of such problems. There was, for instance, one little old woman who worked in the laundry, and who always came in with a big lunch basket. No one could understand why she needed such a large container for her lunch, but as time went on the Sanitarium housekeeper began to notice that they were losing towels and pillow slips. Their investigation pointed to the laundry worker. They found that she actually brought little or no lunch at all, but that she left work at the end of the day with her basket heavily loaded with linens.

The lessons in frugality and thrift which Harry had learned in medical school and which his father had taught him in his early Ohio days were largely responsible, he feels, for later financial success in establishing hospitals around the world. "One who doesn't learn to guard his pennies will never learn how to save the dollars," he insists. "To me, this has been an important lesson in the stewardship of life."

XIV

CONQUERING NEW FIELDS

IT WAS AT Washington Sanitarium during the First World War that Harry Miller got his start in delicate thyroid surgery which led to his world-wide fame as a goiter surgeon. Doing additional postgraduate study after finishing his stint at Johns Hopkins, Dr. Miller spent some time with the noted surgeon George Washington Crile at his Cleveland clinic. No sooner had Miller returned to Washington than a lady with a large goiter came to his office. "That first patient responded well," the doctor recalls, "and I quickly learned that thyroid patients advertise you not only by word of mouth but by the little scar on their necks and the fact that they no longer have bulging eyes or neck line. She made an uneventful recovery and, as women often do, spread the news abroad. Soon a stream of patients was making its way into my office with bulging eyes, excited nerves, or with tumor masses on their necks."

Miller's first twenty-four thyroidectomies were successful, and it was such an unusual record for that time that he was asked to present a paper before the Montgomery County Medical Society of Maryland. He planned to call it "Twenty-five Successful Thyroidectomies"—a dramatic title because the death rate for thyroid patients was high in those days. But alas, his twenty-fifth patient, afflicted with an exophthalmic goiter, had a serious reaction to the anesthetic, and finally succumbed.

In general, Dr. Miller's success was so remarkable—the mortality rate of his patients in his early days of thyroid surgery was an astonishingly low four per cent—that his fame spread along the eastern seaboard, and Washington Sanitarium became a thyroid center. Eventually the Sanitarium grew to a modern two-hundred-fifty-bed institution, with most of the early improvements financed by the fees for thyroid surgery.

Harry Miller learned much in those days, not alone concerning operating technique, but especially about aftercare, the particular hazard of thyroid surgery. The unfortunate outcome of his twenty-fifth thyroidectomy spurred him on to work out a system of hydrotherapy with the use of cold packs and compresses, which resulted in the saving of many patients who might otherwise have been lost. Subsequently, it became well known, through medical literature, that aftercare is at least half the battle with surgery involving toxic goiters.

Surgeons came from many medical centers to the Sanitarium's thyroid clinic to learn more about the activity of the thyroxine on the heat centers of the body. Many of them believed that when the heart was beating so rapidly from the thermal reaction they should still administer digitalis, which was the standard medication for any heart irregularity in those days. Harry Miller, the researcher, proved that that was explicitly not the thing to do. The heart was already overstimulated. It demanded a therapy which would slow down the heartbeat. The discovery brought prestige to the hospital and greatly contributed to Dr. Miller's ultimate record of less than one-half of one per cent fatalities out of more than six thousand thyroidectomies. Thyroid surgery became less feared, and as a result many patients began to seek help in earlier stages of their affliction.

Successful surgery, as any surgeon knows, involves more than aftercare. And the surgical record of Harry Miller, probably unexcelled in medical annals, is no exception. He constantly practiced exercises demanding finger skills. To maintain and increase his manual dexterity he would, for instance, tie knots around buttons, with his hands inside a tin can or small paper sack. No less important were his knowledge of anatomy and his ability to work rapidly. On one occasion he performed a Caesarean section in forty-five seconds. Preparations in the operating room, Miller held from his earliest days, are of great importance. He refused to allow a large number of witnesses in the operating area, although that had been the common practice in his student days under Dr. John Harvey Kellogg. Miller believed that fewer participants meant less contamination.

At a later time, during a medical convention in Shanghai, a number of surgeons asked Dr. Miller for a demonstration of a series of thyroid operations. One of the cases selected was unusually difficult, a thyroid so large that it extended from the tip of the ear down to, and somewhat under, the breastbone. The operation began as usual with local anesthetic. All proceeded well, and Dr. Miller was about to close up the very long incision necessitated by so extensive a goiter. Suddenly a ligature slipped on the superior thyroid artery and there in front of a large crowd assembled in the operating theater the blood spurted like a fountain. Calmly placing his finger at the bleeder and carrying a hemostat along with his finger, the doctor gently located the artery, clamped it off, and stopped the bleeding. Miller apologized to the crowd for the mishap, saying that he was embarrassed for the hemorrhage in their presence. The leading surgeon in the group assured him that he need not apologize.

"We admire your steady nerve," he said, "and the deliberate way you ran your finger up and placed the clamp on the right artery. We are well aware that you had the carotid artery, the jugular vein, and a number of large vessels running right through that area. Almost any surgeon might have become excited and clamped one of them off, and lost his patient."

The other doctors agreed, and one added:

"To us, the accident was the most illuminating part of the whole demonstration. When everything goes well in surgery there isn't much for observers to learn, but when they see a surgeon put to the test as you were here today, it creates great admiration."

Harry Miller's contribution to modern thyroid surgery and its aftercare, especially in connection with thermal reactions, has helped save thousands of lives. For, as skilled surgeons have studied his discoveries and learned his techniques, fatalities from thyroid surgery have fallen from more than fifty per cent to less than one per cent.

A physician not infrequently must be many things to many people: counselor, minister, diagnostician, psychiatrist, comforter, friend. The firm faith that it is God who heals—that the physician is but the instrument of God—has enabled Harry Miller, like many other doctors, to meet the heavy demands of his profession.

There arrived at Washington Sanitarium one day a prominent Presbyterian clergyman who sought a medical opinion from Dr. Daniel H. Kress, formerly of the American Medical Missionary College and a noted specialist in nervous diseases. Dr. Kress discovered, upon examination, that the patient had a diseased colon, and to that and the resultant toxemia he attributed the minister's general nervousness and melancholy. Surgery was necessary, in the opinion of Kress, and he sent the patient to Miller. The clergyman readily assented to the operation.

"When can you do it?" he asked Dr. Miller almost enthusiastically.

"I think we can get you ready today and operate tomorrow," Miller volunteered.

"That's fine!" the minister replied with a smile.

Seldom had the doctor seen a patient respond so promptly to medical advice. Usually, even in connection with simple surgery, Miller had to talk it over with the patient, and encourage him.

Then often the patient would send for members of his family, and they in turn would discuss the proposition with the doctor. Yet this was a major operation—in those days colon surgery was considered particularly hazardous—and the man showed no reluctance. Indeed, he seemed eager for it.

"The quicker the better," said the preacher as he walked out of the doctor's office.

Miller operated the next day. The minister's recovery was excellent, and he was soon off to resume his preaching.

Some time later he returned to Miller's office.

"Doctor, you looked very strangely at me when I first came to you. Remember after you advised surgery, and I told you to go ahead and do it?"

Dr. Miller remembered well.

"I'll tell you why," the minister continued, with a big smile. "I was suffering from such tremendous depression that I had decided to commit suicide. I did not want to disgrace my family at home so I came up here. I climbed out on the window sill in my room, thinking to jump and end it all. But I was just too big a coward. There was no way that I could think of to get rid of myself. But when you showed me the picture of that diseased colon and told me you would have to cut a big section out of it, I thought surely that would be my end—going to sleep under the anesthetic would be the easiest way to die. That's the reason I consented so promptly. Then, at the operating table you prayed for me, and I didn't know what to think. Well, your prayer has been answered. I am a new man, full of courage and hope."

Back in his Tennessee home the clergyman told of his restoration to health—physical and mental—and soon many persons from the area were flocking to Washington Sanitarium. Later on, Dr. LeRoy Coolidge, a Miller colleague, established a hospital in Greenville, Tennessee. It is there today—an institution sponsored by the Seventh-day Adventist Church, but in a very real sense a testimony to the witness of a Presbyterian minister.

Washington, D.C., businessman and Baptist layman, Stanley Powers, who was Dr. Miller's secretary in the early twenties, recites many instances of the doctor's skillful and selfless medical ministry. One story concerns a Florida millionaire who, bedridden for months, had spent tens of thousands of dollars going to the nation's top medical authorities. Then he received word via the grapevine of the almost unbelievable Washington Sanitarium cures, and without delay he went by special coach to Washington.

As Powers tells the story: "He arrived on a stretcher. Pain-racked and apparently a hopeless case, he was so bound up with rheumatism and other complications that he could not walk or even stand up. Dr. Miller gave him a careful examination, including the full laboratory routine of that day, and then looked down in his typically casual way at his outstretched patient. 'Well, friend, you're not in bad shape at all,' Miller said. 'The chances are you will be on your feet in a week or two.'

"The incredulity of the man was obvious to Harry Miller. As if to forestall an expression of doubt, the doctor added slowly, 'I know what you're thinking, but do what we tell you, and you will be up soon.' After an intensive series of hydrotherapy treatments to stimulate circulation, Dr. Miller had the patient brought into surgery where he quickly took out the man's tonsils and adenoids, which had been the source of general toxemia. In a week the man was on his feet, and in ten days he was ready to leave.

"The gentleman paid his bill and then came into our office. With some of the warmest, kindest words of appreciation and affection I have ever heard, I saw him press into Dr. Miller's hand an un-soiled, starch-stiff thousand-dollar bill, the first I had ever seen. I thought how wonderful for Miller to receive this, for the doctor had a family and his total salary with allowances, I knew, was only forty-four dollars a week. But a moment later he turned and handed the greenback to me. 'Here, Stan,' he said, 'take this down to the cashier.'

"That was Harry Miller. I know for a fact that he even had his ten-cent personal telephone calls deducted from his salary check, and from all those remarkable gifts of money, he did not keep a red cent for himself. He was strictly God's man and man's friend."

The steadily increasing flow of patients to Washington Sanitarium created a new difficulty. What had once been a problem of finances became a problem of space. Extra beds were urgently needed. In 1916, Miller proposed a separate hospital unit primarily for surgical cases, pointing out that they were out of debt and were beginning to build a reserve fund, and that their financial success was due in large measure to the surgery performed there. But he could not get the ear of the governing board, whose members were still very conscious of the fiscal crisis four years before. They could not believe that the Sanitarium's unaccustomed prosperity would continue.

In desperation, Dr. Miller finally decided to go ahead without the consent of the board. He drew up blueprints, had excavations made, and was having the building roofed almost before the board knew what was happening. What, they demanded, did the doctor think he was doing? Did he suppose that a modest monetary surplus from surgical cases could finance a whole new structure?

For three days the board considered the grave situation and the doctor's questionable assumption of authority. Finally, Dr. Miller promised that the building would be paid for within a year. To the board that seemed to be an utterly ridiculous statement, but they voted to go ahead. What else could they do?

By the time the hospital unit was completed several months later, it was paid for in full.

The visionary is sometimes confused with the man of vision, the impractical dreamer with the imaginative genius whose judgment and perseverance support his insight, enabling him to carry out his inner vision of possibilities with adventuresome courage. In his later years in China, when colleagues occasionally thought he was emphasizing medical missions to the exclusion of education and evangelism, Dr. Miller would take them to the ledgers, which usually showed that the other arms of the work were profiting from the medical ministry, and, indeed, thriving to an extent that would not have been possible otherwise.

A frequent visitor and dinner guest at Washington Sanitarium in the twenties was Dr. Alfred Sao Sze, China's ambassador to the United States. Sometimes, along with other guests, the ambassador would join in the daily staff meeting or worship service. He often remarked that he found the spiritual atmosphere at the Sanitarium as healing as the treatments.

One day an appeal from Seventh-day Adventist workers in China reached Dr. Miller. They were planning to build a sanitarium in Shanghai, but a local official would not put his stamp to the land deeds in order to legalize the transfer of the property to the Church. Construction could not proceed, of course, without title to the land, so Miller presented the matter to the ambassador in Washington.

"Your problem is that he is a petty little official and, like all of the rest of them, he wants a handout," Dr. Sao Sze said knowingly. "There is little I can do about changing him. But I'll tell you what I *will* do. I will give you a letter to my friend Mayor Kuo T'ai-chi of Shanghai, who is also in charge of the land office. I am sure you would just as soon have his stamp as that of a little bureaucrat."

A few weeks later Harry Miller was on his way back to China at the call of the Church. As soon as he arrived in Shanghai, he made his way quickly to the mayor, who in a matter of minutes placed the necessary seal on the deed.

XV

RETURN TO THE ORIENT

THE MILLERS' RETURN to the Orient in 1925 was a far cry from Harry's first adventure twenty-two years before. To their four children—Clarence had been born in 1915—China was a strange new world. Neither seventeen-year-old Maude nor fifteen-year-old Ethel could remember the land they had left fourteen years earlier. The two boys had never seen it. For them, accustomed to their comfortable little Maryland farm, China provided a striking contrast. To Harry and Marie, the well-loved old country also presented many new things.

With the twentieth century came an era of change for this ancient land. In 1912, the Manchus were brushed aside and the Chinese Republic was established, with Sun Yat-sen as the first president. To many educated Chinese the Kuomintang, the party of Sun Yat-sen, appeared to be ushering in better days. But the rising tide of nationalism and the emergence of Chinese Communism following the First World War brought only strife and division. On March 12, 1925, shortly before the Millers' return, Sun Yat-sen died. However, a new star was rising—that of Chiang Kai-shek, ardent admirer of Sun Yat-sen who was to become, posthumously, Chiang's brother-in-law.

Not all of the changes so apparent to Harry and Marie Miller were political. Generous American supporters were determined to give Dr. Miller every advantage in his new start in China. Dr. Henry Harrower, who owned a pharmaceutical business near Los Angeles, provided twenty thousand dollars. The Washington Sanitarium board supplied laboratory and X-ray technicians, and the wives of the men were nurses. The board also sent a ten-thousand-dollar gift.

With the guidance of missionary E. C. Wood, architect and builder, the construction of Shanghai Sanitarium progressed rapidly. One thing had long puzzled Miller about construction in China, and he found the riddle still existed when Shanghai Sanitarium was being built. Whenever a unit was nearly completed, the contractors passed word around that they were losing money. Yet they apparently enjoyed building for Miller and Wood, and kept coming back for more contracts. The doctor could not understand how they could be losing money all the time, and still stay in business. Then one day Wood explained it to him:

"You see, when a Chinese builder makes his bid he of course estimates his profit. Let's say he figures on making fifty thousand dollars. Then he finds out after he has paid all his bills that he has made only twenty-five thousand dollars. He's looking for a little sympathy—and a little more profit. The fact is, these people like to work for us because they make money and always receive their payment promptly."

To understand many of the problems confronting Dr. Miller at that time requires some knowledge of the city's political situation. Shanghai was one of the most strangely governed cities in the world. The government of China had no regular control. Western powers—notably Britain—and Japan had jurisdiction over the International Settlement, which included three-quarters of the city. France controlled its own French Settlement. The remaining scattered pockets of the city were in Chinese hands.

Those conditions produced a chaotic situation. Political unrest was rife, uprisings were legion, actual attacks by foreign foes not

uncommon—and small wonder. Bandit raids and kidnapings occurred frequently. Outlaws usually seized men or children, took
them to an undisclosed spot, and tortured them until the ransom
demanded from relatives was forthcoming. Often, persons who
were released reported that the desperadoes had shown them a
man's heart excised from some unfortunate victim who had tried
to resist.

On one occasion a group of missionaries and tourists were riding the famed Blue Express between Shanghai and Peking when
it was derailed, in clever fashion, by a gang of thugs. They
herded the passengers, among whom were Mrs. John D. Rockefeller II and a score of well-to-do Americans, into the hills, keeping them there for the better part of three weeks. When the
outlaws were apprehended later, they were quizzed on their
technique.

"How did you learn that trick of derailing the train?"

"We saw it in an American Western in the Peking cinema,"
was the reply.

Harry Miller's life in China was dedicated to helping the Chinese help themselves—to raising the health and sanitary standards
of the nation, to making it possible for these objectives to be ac-
complished with less and less dependence on foreigners, to making
these benefits available to poor and rich alike. An interesting commentary on the times is found in the selection of the site for
Shanghai Sanitarium. While still in Washington, Dr. Miller had
been consulted on the matter. He wanted to locate it in the country, believing a rural setting to be good medicine in itself. However, owing to bandit scares, the wealthy would seldom leave the
city. Miller compromised by building the Sanitarium only slightly
beyond the edge of the city.

Those were the days—when the hospital was under construction
—that the doctor had to stand night watch to keep the building
supplies intact. The marauders were so ruthless that no respectable
Chinese would stay out after dark.

As unit after unit was added to the Sanitarium, Dr. Miller divided his time between surgery and soliciting for funds. Of the two hundred fifty beds in the completed hospital, two hundred were for charity patients or for those who could pay only part of their expenses. From the day of the formal opening of Shanghai Sanitarium—January 1, 1928—patients crowded the doors. Most of them were charity cases.

One time a Sanitarium nurse, attracted by a muted whimper, picked up a day-old baby boy from a Shanghai refuse heap and took him to the Sanitarium. He was the fifth infant in as many weeks to be brought in by one of the nurses. The other four babies were girls, however. Chinese seldom abandon children except in utter desperation, but to abandon a male child was almost unheard of. Perhaps for that reason the staff especially treasured the little baby boy from the refuse heap, whom they named Dotsiang. He rapidly grew into a healthy child, and within two years he was adopted by a prominent Chinese family.

He was but one of many fortunate youngsters from Miller's "Baby Boarding House," as the children's ward was sometimes called. Babies, especially the homeless ones, had an inside track to Dr. Miller's heart, and the Chinese knew this. On occasion the doctor found abandoned babies in his own front yard, usually lowered over the compound wall in the dead of night. A wail sounding much like the crying of a stray kitten would awaken Miller, and he would don his slippers and quilted robe to investigate—usually returning with another orphan for the Sanitarium.

Of the Sanitarium, Dr. Miller says: "Contrary to our early fears when we were building it, the Sanitarium *was* apparently safer than the city, whether in uncertain peace or in war. One wealthy Chinese, D. C. Chuan, occasionally came from Manila to Shanghai on business. His friends were always fearful that if he stayed in town it would be an invitation to kidnaping. So on his Shanghai visits they paid the Sanitarium well for a suite of rooms—and medical attention—where he carried on his business until his ship returned en route to Manila."

Only persons who have lived in the midst of an ancient civilization in violent transition can understand those days in China. Despite Chiang Kai-shek's efforts to bring order out of the despotic legacy of the Manchu dynasty, the times were against him. The festering political sores of China were being contaminated by urbanization, poverty, uncertainty of the future, and international mistrust. That hotbed served well the needs of Communism, and eventually China was split asunder by conflicting political views.

Many members of the foreign colony were drawn into the controversies. But Harry Miller, the surgeon, was determined to give no cause for gossip by alignment with any one of the ideologies or political groups. It was an especially precarious tightrope he walked at Shanghai Sanitarium.

XVI

NO RECIPES IN CHINA

SHANGHAI SANITARIUM'S PROBLEM was not lack of patients. They came by the hundreds. But, as has been said, most of them were charity cases; the Sanitarium could not survive unless patients who could pay came also.

If the roads to the Sanitarium were repaired, someone pointed out, wealthy patients might come.

And come they did.

One of the first was the widow of Charlie Soong, from whom Harry Miller had rented space for his printing establishment in earlier days. Madame Soong, a beloved and highly respected woman, had many visitors. Soon a number of them registered as patients. After the capital was moved from Peking south to Nanking in 1928, many Government leaders went to the Sanitarium for treatment or meals, and on several occasions they held cabinet meetings in the parlor.

Also, Miller received frequent calls for medical consultation with persons in the Central Government at Nanking. Whenever he returned from the north, inquisitive guests closed in on him for information on the Nationalists. Some were more snoopy than a Chihuahua puppy and just as nervous—about their political enemies. The same happened to a lesser degree at Nanking—a curiosity about the doctor's patients in Shanghai. His reply was the same to all: "My business is medicine, not politics. You know I would not last five minutes as a politician, and I wouldn't be here to treat you now." Eventually, the institution became a modern hospital with a nursing school enrolling students from all over the Far East.

The problems of the developmental period were not without their humorous aspects. The Sanitarium personnel had had no previous experience in feeding such large and diverse groups. Patients and guests came from North, South, and West China, and each section was as different in its dietary habits as any two countries of the East. Because many of the patients were thin and weak from malnutrition, as would be expected of persons from destitute areas, the Sanitarium established what they called a "universal diet."

Its core was whole-wheat bread and half-polished rice, and a nutritious milk which Dr. Miller devised from the soybean, for animal milk was not readily available. The staff and most of the patients responded well, gaining substantially in weight and body tone. Yet, Dr. Miller had reason to believe that the cooks were not imaginative enough to help him to convince some patients of the advantages of vegetables over meat. Although most Chinese were vegetarians, oftentimes the rich and the foreigners were not. To make their diet attractive, a provincial Chinese cook would not do. Harry Miller, the nutritionist, was convinced from a preventive-medicine point of view that the "firsthand" food in vegetables was of sufficiently greater value than the "secondhand" nutriments of meat to justify his securing an American chef.

While Miller was on a trip to America, a number of his friends around Washington, D.C., sang the praises of Ed Meisler, the head chef at Washington Missionary College (the Foreign Mission Seminary of earlier years). He told Meisler about some of the problems—he dared not tell all—and asked Ed if he would undertake the establishment of the dining room at Shanghai Sanitarium. Ed and his wife agreed to it.

When Meisler arrived in China, Miller told him frankly:

"Ed, we are having an awful time feeding these people, especially the rich, because each one of them wants to have his own food brought in twice a day from restaurants downtown. By the time it gets here it is cold. We want them to follow our diet if they are to get well, and we're laying the whole matter in your lap."

"Maybe the problem is bigger than you think," Ed replied. "First, I'll have to learn how to cook Chinese food." Already he had been experimenting with cereals, vegetables, fruits, and nuts, but he knew little about Chinese seasonings.

"How about looking in on some Buddhist cooks and developing a cookbook for us?" the doctor suggested hopefully. The Chinese Buddhist restaurants served only meatless dishes, and were noted for their top-notch chefs. Ed responded with typical enthusiasm, and cooking lessons were arranged. He learned how the Chinese use soybeans, wheat gluten, and other sources of protein for variety or when they tire of eggs.

Several days later, Dr. Miller asked Ed how things were going.

"So-so," he answered limply, obviously without the eagerness of the week before.

"What's the matter, Ed," the doctor pressed.

"Well, Doc, I'm really puzzled," he replied simply. "Why don't you come down? It's a lot easier to see than for me to tell it."

So the doctor went with him. True to Ed's words, it was much easier seen than explained. Miller had been in many Chinese restaurants, but he had never lingered to watch the cook go through the complete routine. On the shelf in front of his big cooking pan, the chef had rows of spices and seasonings, such as ginger, salt, caramel, starch water, pepper, and monosodium glutamate. On a long table behind them was a variety of ingredients

—peas, string beans, soybean curd, Chinese cabbage, fresh ginger, onions, garlic, mushrooms, bean sprouts, gluten, and other foods, including a variety of well-chopped leafy vegetables.

The men watched with intense interest as the chef started dropping ingredients into the big kettle suspended over the open fire. First, some oil which he heated, then a handful of leafy vegetables to wilt in the oil. Next, a bit of water to cook the vegetables a little more, whereupon he covered the big skillet. A few minutes later he added the soy cheese, gluten, some peas, and a few noodles. It all depended, the chef explained, on the effect he wanted. But he didn't define "effect." The variety of dishes was endless, and they were often custom-made to the patrons' tastes.

After cooking this mixture for a while, the chef began the elaborate seasoning routine. There was a pinch of this, a sprinkle of that, and a dash of something else. Then he took a spoon and tasted it. Something was lacking, and he always seemed to know what it was. He reached for more garlic, threw in a little caramel for coloring, mixed it thoroughly, and tasted it again. This process he repeated a half-dozen times with various seasonings, poured out the entree ready for the hungry diner, and then started all over again on another kind of dish in the same pan.

Ed looked up, half in challenge and half in mirth.

"Well, Doctor, will you write that down?"

He was right. It was impossible to copy even one Chinese recipe, much less to make a cookbook.

"You see," Ed explained, "cooking with them is an art, not a science."

Although they never cooked by exact proportions, they did cook by principles. For example, they had a certain order for mixing ingredients, and they did time the wilting process of the vegetables.

Not only is Chinese cooking an art, but perhaps in no country does eating play a more important part in the national culture. Seldom is a big business venture completed without a feast. The chefs wait until all the guests have arrived before beginning to cook. The food must be served steaming hot, for by nature Chinese foods cool quickly. Ordinarily the guests sit drinking tea and chewing on watermelon seeds while awaiting the dinner, which usually lasts at least three hours and frequently has twelve courses.

In such Chinese feasts the host and hostess eat little. Their principal concern is to see that their guests' plates are kept filled, all the while in a gesture of humility lamenting that they have no food to offer. It is the role of the guests, in turn, to apologize for their lack of vocabulary to express adequately their pleasure and appreciation.

The Chinese custom of tea drinking grew out of the fact that the Chinese had to boil their water to avoid such diseases as typhoid, cholera, or dysentery, and they used flower petals or plant leaves to flavor it. Seldom did they use tea leaves of the type known to Westerners. In short, China's diet developed largely as a result of specific needs and limitations. In the China that Harry Miller lived in, the scarcity of food in the great majority of homes was real. The masses lived from hand to mouth, stomachs seldom filled, no more than one good meal a day.

The quaint rituals of feasting were colorless compared with the old Chinese customs at the turn of the century. In the early years, when Harry Miller approached a shopkeeper for even so much as a bit of thread or a piece of cloth there was an opening dialogue which he engaged in, in all seriousness, but which always appealed to his sense of humor.

"What is your venerable age?" was invariably the first query.

"I have grown up in vain for thirty years," was an acceptable answer.

"And how many illustrious sons do you have?"

"I have but two little girl monkeys," the doctor would say, playing along.

"I am sorry that my shop is so worthless, empty, and unkept," the Chinese would continue.

"Not at all," Miller would reply. "I was just admiring your prosperous business and calculating your stupendous fortune!"

"No, you are talking to a miserable failure," the shopkeeper would insist in tragicomic style, and would then proceed to pour his guest a big cup of tea while putting only a few drops in his tiny demitasse. At that point, Miller would pick up the big teapot and insist on filling the shopkeeper's cup before dickering for his ten cents' worth of dry goods.

Some foreigners thought this was hypocritical, and turned away from the little game. But to the Chinese it was not hypocrisy, nor was it without reason. The practice existed as an expression of humility in the context of an ancient civilization understood by few Westerners.

XVII

HIGH FINANCE

BUILDING INSTITUTIONS over a nation as vast as China was an awesome undertaking. But unshakable in their belief in a Power greater than their own, Harry Miller and his co-workers undertook one project after another in the twenties and thirties. Their purpose was to bring the healing ministry of Christ to all—the poor as well as the rich. If building was a problem, maintaining and operating the institutions was an even greater challenge. In the generosity of men and women of wealth the missionaries found fulfillment of the promise of the prophet Isaiah that "strangers shall build up thy walls." Furthermore, the strangers became their friends, for where one's treasure is there will his heart be also.

There was, for example, T'ang Shao-i who had been governor general of Korea and premier of China. He received prominence as the premier who held the country together when the Empress Dowager fled Peking at the outbreak of the Boxer Rebellion. He it was who went to Sian and brought the Empress back to make her sign new treaties between China and the foreign powers.

T'ang was still revered as senior statesman of the nation. When he was at Shanghai Sanitarium, for periodic check-ups or because of illness, he always occupied the corner room on the third floor, one of the best rooms. Opposite his room was a surgical ward.

One day when he was strolling in the hall he dropped in to see a surgical patient who had caught his eye. In the evening when Dr. Miller made his rounds, T'ang asked him to sit down.

"How much are you receiving for that fellow," he inquired, identifying the patient across the hall.

"We probably won't charge him anything," Miller replied.

"I knew you couldn't get anything from him," was T'ang's rejoinder. "He has a family of ten to support on a pittance of a salary. You have many patients like this?"

"We take everyone we can without discrimination," the surgeon told him, "but we are always limited by the space we have."

A few days later, T'ang called Harry Miller in again, and without preliminaries handed him a check for ten thousand dollars as a gift to extend his clinical work for Shanghai's poor. He was the same T'ang Shao-i who admired the democracy of America because he had known it through a dear friend—Herbert Hoover. The medical missionary program profited immensely from the example set by the American whose heart had gone out to the hungry of the world.

Madame Chiang Kai-shek and her sister, Madame H. H. Kung, were regular callers at Shanghai Sanitarium. They especially liked the steambaths and other hydrotherapy treatments. One day Madame Chiang suffered an attack of appendicitis, and an examination indicated that surgery was advisable.

"I would like my operation early in the morning, if you please, Dr. Miller," she requested. At her suggestion he also called in Dr. Wei Ling-nu, her former physician, to assist. Madame Chiang recovered quickly from the operation and soon left the hospital. A few weeks later she returned to the Sanitarium to see Harry Miller.

"I know you never make large charges, Dr. Miller," she said, "even for the rich. But you haven't sent me any bill at all."

The American believed that Madame had a keen sense of

justice and in due time would pay what she thought the operation was worth. He also knew that she had been very upset when a dentist charged her five hundred dollars for dental work worth no more than fifty dollars.

At her urging, Miller sent a bill for about two hundred dollars, including surgery and hospitalization. That she paid. A few weeks later, while at the Sanitarium on one of her routine visits, Madame Chiang called the doctor to her room.

"Dr. Miller, I have something in the drawer for you," she said, pulling out a big stack of Chinese notes. "Use this for your new clinic."

Back in his office, the doctor counted the money; she had given three thousand dollars. Madame Chiang is typical of the wealthy Chinese, who are almost invariably liberal and who much prefer to give voluntarily and without pressure.

Su Mei-chang, a well-to-do woman lawyer, was the wife of Wei Tao-ming, governor of Formosa and later ambassador to the United States. After a siege of chronic tonsillitis she went to the Sanitarium for a simple tonsillectomy. She, too, received no bill. She was so grateful for the relief the surgery had brought her, however, that she sent a thousand-dollar gift, and also mentioned to many of China's leaders the "wonderful" care she had received. Shortly after that, she contributed another two thousand dollars, and still other gifts at later periods.

F. L. H. Pott, president of St. John's University, established in Shanghai by the Protestant Episcopal Church of the United States, was married to a fine Chinese woman. Mrs. Pott's sister, Dr. Wong, professor of gynecology and obstetrics at St. John's Medical College, became seriously ill with an exophthalmic goiter and called Miller in. She was emaciated and weak, a poor surgical risk.

"I'm afraid of surgery, Dr. Miller," she told him with fear in her eyes.

"Yes, I know, but what other hope have we?"

"That's right, there's no alternative, is there?" She understood the situation well.

Miller took her into the hospital, and because her weak heart could not tolerate a general anesthetic, gave her a local one. Conscious of what was going on, she was restless and talkative throughout the surgery.

"Oh, let me die in peace," she would repeat. "I am dying, why keep on?"

Not only did the surgeon have to listen to that, but her nervous movements made the delicate throat surgery exceedingly difficult. Here again, Harry Miller attributed a remarkable recovery to the help of Providence. Under professional reciprocity he, of course, made no charges. Some time later, one of the hospital solicitors was making a routine call for funds and asked Dr. Wong if she would care to contribute one hundred dollars for the clinic building.

"No, I don't think so," Dr. Wong said, stalling for fun. Then a few moments later she brought out her surprise, a check for two thousand dollars.

A middle-aged Chinese woman, injured in an automobile wreck, was taken to Shanghai Sanitarium unconscious. Judged by reason of her very ordinary clothes to be of no more than average circumstances, she was placed in one of the less expensive rooms. It was a serious orthopedic case with multiple fractures, and her arm had to be carefully set and wired. Her recovery took weeks, but she seemed unusually grateful for the care she received.

"They have saved my life here," she would tell her fellow patients.

After her release from the hospital she paid a modest fee, but made up her mind she wanted to do something especially for Dr. Miller. A friend of hers had suggested a watch, but Miller demurred. He already had one and, besides, he preferred not to accept anything personally. Mrs. Woo was, however, a determined woman. One day she took the doctor to the studio of an Italian marble sculptor before informing him that he was there to have a plaster cast made. She planned to erect the statue on the Sanitarium's front lawn. "I told her as politely and vigorously as possible that I simply could not allow that," says Dr. Miller with a smile. "And I added that seeing me out there at night would frighten people—or at least make me shiver from the cold."

On another pretext Mrs. Woo took the doctor to a bronze worker to have a casting made, to be placed in the Sanitarium hall. When he refused again, she became angry. However, she still needed treatment and she continued to return to the Sanitarium until she recovered the normal use of her arm. A short while later she handed Dr. Miller a check for twenty thousand dollars to build a new dormitory for the head nurses, on the condition that he consent to have his photograph in the foyer and to name the building "Miller Hall."

This time the doctor agreed, and Mrs. Woo saved face. After the building was under way she took Miller to the bank and gave him the balance needed to finish the construction. But, for the dedicated surgeon, the greatest reward was Mrs. Woo's subsequent acceptance of the Christian faith.

The Philippines contributed to the hospital work in China in a unique way. Dr. Miller went to Manila Sanitarium at intervals to perform series of operations arranged for in advance by Harry Steinmetz and Chai Vizcarra, doctors at Manila. There were always some well-to-do patients, and their fees were divided, half going to medical missions in the Philippines and half to China. Miller was curious to know how Dr. Vizcarra could tell which persons could pay and which could not. Most of the wealthy people paid their fees without question. Some, however, aware that the mission hospital charged little or nothing for charity patients, left their automobiles at home and arrived at Manila Sanitarium in caromatas (quaint little pony-drawn truck carts), hoping to qualify for charity.

"How can you spot them?" Miller asked the Filipino doctor one day.

"Well," Vizcarra said, "first, I check them for jewelry. If they have taken that off, I ask them to stick out their tongues in a sort of preliminary examination. If they have gold fillings in their teeth, I know they have money."

The remarkable financial success of Dr. Miller's ventures through the years is largely attributable to the character of the man himself. Single-minded in his devotion to building up the health of both oriental and occidental, the missionary doctor has given most of his fees, honoraria, and royalties from books* either to the institutions of his Church or to nutritional research. Close associates estimate conservatively that in professional fees alone Harry Miller has turned over more than two million five hundred thousand dollars.

While many of the prominent physicians in Shanghai and other oriental cities enriched themselves through excessive fees, he accepted only the standard subsistence salary provided to missionaries. Many leading doctors were driven about in chauffeured sedans, indicative of status, but Harry Miller usually drove a topless old Dodge or an Oakland touring car. Rather than live in a stylish compound, as did many successful medical practitioners, Miller was known widely for his preference for "living like the Chinese" in a simple cottage on the hospital grounds. Always available to his patients, regardless of social status or creed, he was known throughout China as a servant of God and a friend to man.

* Miller's most widely distributed book, *Health and Longevity*, was written in Chinese, and has been translated into many languages.

XVIII

FACING THE MEDICAL BOARDS

FOR A PHYSICIAN whose practice encircles the globe, life is an unending trail of medical licenses. Be it for a license to practice in one of the states of the United States or in a foreign country, the unnerving experience of facing a medical board is inevitable.

About 1928, some twenty-six years after he had graduated from medical school, Dr. Miller was being called repeatedly from China to the Philippines for intensive schedules of highly specialized surgery. Since he went by invitation of Filipino specialists, no thought was given to his writing the Philippine medical examinations. The local doctors did not mind so long as he did only charity work. But one day a wealthy Filipino jeweler offered Miller over one thousand dollars for an operation. Dr. Miller performed the surgery and accepted the fee, which he immediately donated toward the establishment of Manila Sanitarium. Nevertheless, there was some professional jealousy, which ended in Dr. Miller's sitting for the examinations. It was with considerable trepidation that he agreed to do so. The Philippine examinations covered sixteen subjects and required four days to write. Taking the examinations along with Miller was another American, a young physician by the name of Horace Hall, newly out of the College of Medical Evangelists. The weather was almost unbearably humid. Miller was so certain he would not obtain a passing grade that he returned to Shanghai without waiting to learn the results.

Later he received a cablegram from his Manila friend, Dr. Harry Steinmetz:

You passed examination. Third highest. Your name and picture in paper. Only man in history of Philippine Medical Board to obtain 100 per cent in any subject. Your 100 per cent in surgery.

Twenty years later when Miller asked to sit for the British medical examinations in Canada he was told flatly by the registrar and secretary of Canada's medical board at Ottawa: "It will be impossible for you to get by the Canadian examination." The registrar pointed out that Dr. Miller was then nearly seventy and that no man more than twenty years out of medical college had ever passed the Canadian examinations. "Nevertheless, the Lord was again good to me," Dr. Miller says. He passed without difficulty, and has since used the license in British territories around the world.

No examinations, however, quite matched those Miller took in order to be licensed by the Japan Medical Association. In 1928, Miller was called to temporary duty at Tokyo Sanitarium and Hospital, an institution which he had helped to establish. It seemed to be the appropriate time to take the examinations, so Miller did, along with Dr. E. E. Getzlaff, a College of Medical Evangelists graduate.

"The examination will be both oral and written," they were advised by the clerk on the medical board.

"In the Japanese language?" they inquired.

"No, you may take it in English," the clerk returned, smiling, the corners of his eyes wrinkling behind his round-rimmed spectacles.

They breathed easily for a moment as they made out application forms. Then the clerk spoke again.

"You will write these examinations for one week, and if you pass—and if you pass, I say," his eyes were twinkling as he spoke, "you will be given an opportunity in about three weeks for spoken questions." He referred to the oral examination to be given—usually in clinical subjects.

A few days later Miller and Getzlaff reported to the Ministry of Health and sat down to the task. The questions were general in content, and uniquely phrased in Japanese English: "Tell extensively about gall-bladder diseases." "What can happen to the colon from diseases?"

Out of his knowledge of oriental psychology, Dr. Miller advised his fellow examinee to write and write and write—the longest essay possible on each subject—on the theory that the amount of writing and the size of the answers would demonstrate to the Japanese examiners that the doctors were well informed.

"At least, we hope that is what they will think," Dr. Getzlaff said skeptically.

Ten days later—ten days of morbid speculation—they received word that they had passed the written examinations and now would be admitted to the "important" part. Meeting at the Ministry of Health at the appointed time, they found three other foreigners—an American woman pediatrician and two Germans—who had also passed their written examinations and were ready to take the orals.

Instead of private examinations, all five doctors were ushered into a cluttered room. In the center of the room on a long library table lay a large assortment of textbooks and journals on biochemistry, going back a full twenty years.

Biochemistry! Dr. Miller's heart sank. Chemistry had been one subject in which he had always felt incompetent, and biochemistry was the part of it which he particularly feared, for it had not been taught in medical schools in his day.

"I will open one of these books or journals to the year of your graduation," the biochemistry professor was saying. "At whatever point I open the book, that subject you will discuss." He illustrated his words by flipping open several journals and a book.

He first called on one of the German physicians. Reaching for a thick tome on the chemistry of the blood, the professor turned haphazardly to a chapter two-thirds of the way through the book. It was on a highly technical aspect of the field, about which, Dr. Miller immediately realized, he knew almost nothing.

"This is really something," he breathed quietly to Getzlaff. "And it takes only one false step in one subject to fail the whole examination."

The first doctor answered adequately, and the professor turned to the second German physician. A current journal was opened for the young doctor. He immediately found himself in great distress.

Third came Dr. Getzlaff, only recently out of medical school. He discussed his subject to the obvious satisfaction of the professor. Now the pressure was on Dr. Miller. What was to happen to him, a senior surgeon of the Far East?

The examiner turned to Miller, pausing a moment as if in respect for the doctor's graying head.

"And what year did you graduate?"

"In 1902," Miller replied simply, in the respectful tone of one oriental answering another.

The professor looked over the long table stacked high with chemistry literature. His little finger, long, sinewy, and crowned with a professorial fingernail fully an inch long, glided over the titles of the books, turned end down.

"Hmmm," he voiced concern, and his finger again went over the titles, this time nervously. "That is very long ago."

"Please do not be concerned about that." Dr. Miller spoke in a gesture of consolation mingled with respect, carefully designed to ingratiate himself with the professor.

"I can find one here in 1907. Would that be all right?"

"Certainly, sir." Dr. Miller was all agreement. "But I want to tell you before you even open this book that I know practically nothing about the subject." He was hoping that his frankness, his experience, and the change in date might arouse enough professorial sympathy to pull him through.

The examiner opened the book to a chapter on "Heat Production." Dr. Miller glanced at the page hopelessly. Then, just as he was about to re-emphasize the futility of the whole situation, his better judgment cautioned him to await the professor's question.

"Tell me what you know about thyroxine," the professor began.

Thyroxine! There were few people in the whole world who knew more about it than Dr. Miller. He quickly and enthusiastically described the hormone, a secretion of the thyroid gland, and the rise in temperature and thermal reaction produced by its over-activity. He had learned little about heat production through chemistry, but as a goiter specialist he knew a great deal about the fevers thyroid surgery produced.

Dr. Miller talked on, minutely describing the amount of thyroxine utilized in milligrams daily, the quantity normally found in thyroid glands—on and on until the professor, deeply impressed with the competency of his examinee, put up his left hand in a gesture of satisfaction and turned to the woman physician.

The rest was anticlimax to Miller and Getzlaff. It was easy now to discover more humor than perplexity in the examination of the capable pediatrician.

"Give me an analysis of cow's milk," the examiner specified after thumbing a journal.

"Which kind of cow's milk?" the woman inquired.

"What do you mean, which kind of cow's milk?" The professor was taken aback.

"Jersey? Holstein? Ayrshire? On what kind of a cow would you like me to give you an analysis?"

The professor was confounded.

"I want to know the analysis of just plain cow's milk." The obviously competent doctor quickly gave him all the necessary answers.

Before long, the examinees were complimenting the professor on his profound ability to discuss articles from French, German, English, and American books and periodicals.

"No doubt you have found us a very poorly informed group," Dr. Miller said in true oriental manner. "You certainly have been generous and gentle with us in this important examination."

The professor left the room temporarily, and five jittery doctors attempted to hide their nervousness with nonchalant conversation. Soon the professor re-entered, exchanging bows with the awkward occidentals.

"I am very pleased to tell you that you have all passed," he announced, his bespectacled countenance dignified and sober. Then, turning to Dr. Miller, his face suddenly seemed to glow as he pushed his horn-rimmed spectacles higher on his nose, and he smiled broadly: "And the oldest passed the best of all."

XIX

A DOCTOR'S CHOICE

EARLY ONE MORNING IN 1930, Harry Miller headed for the Shanghai airport and the ancient one-motored amphibian that would transport him, yo-yo fashion, to Chekiang Province, Foochow, Amoy, Swatow, Hong Kong, and finally, Canton. Crude and risky as it was, the old box-kite saved many a day—and scores of lives— in Miller's pressing surgery schedules. Dr. Floyd Bates, a graduate of the College of Medical Evangelists, had worked hard to build the new Canton Sanitarium. During its first weeks of operation, Bates had lined up for Miller a series of twenty or more surgery cases, most of them thyroid and some of them urgent.

When Miller landed at Canton he was handed a message by a courier from the provincial governor:

Wang Ching-wei shot in head and back. You are needed for emergency operation. Generalissimo has ordered plane for your immediate travel to Nanking.

He passed the note to Dr. Bates, who was there to meet him.

"The premier?" Bates asked unbelievingly.

"Yes, the premier," Miller replied. "Apparently an assassination attempt."

Dr. Bates wrung his hands.

"It will be terrible for us if you leave now," he said. "We have all those patients in the hospital, and some can't wait! Besides, if you go without knowing when you will be able to return, all of our patients may leave us."

The senior surgeon understood well his colleague's dilemma. In the Orient, the reputation of a new hospital hinged largely on the initial patient-group. Furthermore, a missionary doctor does not give premier priority over peasant; he ministers equally to all, regardless of rank. Yet the decision was not that simple, for the death of Premier Wang might precipitate war. Turning to the courier, Miller asked what arrangements had been made about the plane. The courier replied that the governor was at that moment rushing to locate one to take the doctor to Shanghai where he would board the Generalissimo's. After scribbling a note for the courier, Miller took Floyd Bates by the elbow as they headed for the Sanitarium.

"We will work until the plane is here," he promised.

Dr. Bates and his staff sprang into action. By the time Dr. Miller was scrubbed, the first patient had been prepared and was nearly under the anesthetic. Surgery proceeded steadily the rest of the afternoon and through the night. By daybreak, the nine most urgent operations had been performed, and Dr. Bates agreed that the others could wait until the surgeon's return from Nanking.

At six o'clock that morning Dr. Miller was off on a China National Airways plane for Shanghai. There, four hours later, he transferred to the Generalissimo's waiting plane. A brief word with the Generalissimo after he reached Nanking, and Miller was taken in to Premier Wang, who had one bullet lodged under his scalp and another in his spine. Following consultation with the staff physicians, Dr. Miller decided to remove the bullet from Wang's head, but not to touch the one in the spine. Thus far there were no indications of paralysis, and although Wang was in pain, to take the bullet from his back would probably paralyze and might kill him.

The scalp surgery was simple, and soon the American was on his way back to Canton. Wang Ching-wei lived uneventfully with his spinal bullet until, a few years later, he left the Generalissimo to become a puppet ruler for the Japanese. He was taken to Tokyo for removal of the second bullet, with promise of "superior" attention, and there died under the surgeon's knife. Surgeons can make wrong decisions, and Dr. Miller claimed no immunity. But he was understandably thankful that his decision at Nanking had not been the one that cost Wang his life.

At Canton, Harry Miller had seen how distressed for lack of operating-room equipment Dr. Bates was, and he knew that there are few situations more disturbing to a surgeon.

"Dr. Miller," Bates had inquired in frustration, "why do they bring doctors out here, and then give them nothing to work with?"

His question spoke volumes, and as medical secretary for the Church's China Division, Miller felt his own responsibility. Floyd Bates had given up fine prospects in America for this unpromising job. He was hard working and efficient, and he wanted to get things under way. While waiting for the hospital construction to be completed, Bates had leased some land and put up temporary bamboo-mat houses for tubercular patients. Yet, despite the valiant and fruitful efforts of Ezra Longway and Mrs. John Oss, the mission's top-notch solicitors, China's shifting economy often created problems.

"I have found that God provides when we need it most," Miller had said to Bates, aware that the reassurance was not of much help.

Not long afterward, when Dr. Miller arrived in the Crown Colony of Hong Kong on a trip from Shanghai, word was waiting for him to call at the home of Sun Fo, whose father was the late Sun Yat-sen. Sun Fo, his wife, their daughters, and their two sons had been patients of Miller's for some years.

"I am so glad you came," the young Madame Sun greeted the doctor with lovely oriental care. Her dark eyes always shone with that peculiarly tender quality of concern often characteristic of well-poised women. "We have been waiting so long for the time when you could come."

After the oriental greetings he was ushered into their carefully furnished, deep-carpeted east room, a precise reflection of the exquisite taste of petite Madame Sun. There Sun Fo revealed the purpose of the call.

"We want you to be godfather for Tsi-ping, our eldest son," he said eagerly, and with a smile.

The missionary was honored beyond expression. Seldom did he enjoy so delightful a repast as Madame Sun set before him that night, graced as it was with the dainty ways of the East and with poignant reminiscences of better days in the Chinese homeland. Before he left, as if to crown honor with gold, Madame Sun pressed in his hand an envelope.

"We have nothing, nothing," she apologized, "to show our gratitude and our esteem."

Dr. Miller felt that the gracious interlude was enough to make anyone feel unworthy. "But when I opened the envelope in my room an hour later," he recalls, "I was utterly unprepared for the gift enclosed—a check for two thousand dollars."

The uniquely Chinese mixture of generosity, tenderness, and love brought unaccustomed tears to his eyes. Here was not only the reward for friendship and service past, but the answer to one physician's doubts and another doctor's prayers. Harry Miller quickly obtained the concurrence of the China Division's president, A. L. Ham, that the greatest need at the moment was for operating equipment for Canton Sanitarium's surgery wing, and, as always, he passed his gift on to "the work."

Although it was a Japanese surgeon's wrong decision that cost one Chinese premier his life, it was the patient himself who made the choice in another case, when Dr. Miller was treating another premier—T'an Yen-kai, one of China's most able statesmen and military leaders.* He was a regular visitor at Shanghai Sanitarium, but this time he was critically ill with nephritis, his body horribly swollen, eyes puffed almost shut, and blood pressure dangerously high. He was known to be a hearty eater, a heavy smoker, and an intemperate connoisseur of wine.

"Diagnosis and treatment were simple, however," says Dr. Miller. "And as long as we had General T'an in the hospital he did well. We knew he was urgently needed as president of China's Executive Yüan—its cabinet—and we undertook radical treatment. We cut off his tobacco and wine completely, and sharply limited his diet. Before long the swelling was gone, and he was up and about. Finally we released him for return to Nanking."

Fearing Premier T'an's reversion to his old habits, his Government associates asked Miller to construct a little sanitarium unit at T'an's home and to send a nurse to keep an eye on him. The surgeon, taking with him a male nurse, went to Nanking, designed a treatment unit including steam bath complete with boiler, and then prescribed the treatment.

"General T'an," Miller admonished, "if you cut out some of your pet habits, especially smoking and drinking, and follow our routine, you will probably live many years."

"Dr. Miller," he answered, looking up at the American more in pity than in rebuttal, "life does not consist in length only."

Miller says: "I agreed in my heart that each man has his own dream of the full life, but T'an Yen-kai's wisdom in affairs of state was needed that his nation also might have the joy of life. I gave the nurse instructions and left.

"Back in Shanghai a few weeks later I received an urgent phone call from T. V. Soong, treasurer of China, and brother of Madame Chiang Kai-shek: 'T'an Yen-kai is in a coma. The weather is poor for flying so we are ordering a special train for you. Can you come to Nanking today?'

---

* No relation to the General T'an who served as the Young Marshal's chief of staff.

"I made preparations and went to the station to meet the train. But before the train arrived, Dr. Soong called me at the station. 'Cancel your trip,' he said somberly, 'the premier is dead.' His death was a deep disappointment to the Government and to me. But sometimes a doctor is helpless when faced with a patient's choice."

XX

TRAVEL BY PRESUMPTION

TRAVEL IN THE ORIENT was fraught with constant adventure and some danger. The topless old Dodge in which the doctor drove around Shanghai often drew wry jokes from his fellow Americans. It matched the Orient well, for it not only was slow to get going, but did almost everything backwards, from the occidental point of view. Just as the oriental cabinet makers pull their saws and planes instead of pushing them, so it was with the old Dodge. The gear-shift system was the reverse of that of any other American car.

One time—in the early thirties—Dr. Miller headed for Kansu Province and Chinghai with mission aides Harold Shultz and Johann Effenburg to decide upon a location for a new mission. Previously, Miller had journeyed into that area only by donkey cart and on foot. In fact, travel had been so dangerous in the early days that Miller had further abetted the pigtail garb of his first years in China by camouflaging his face with a coat of diluted iodine. With his high cheekbones he had thus passed more easily for a Chinese in the bandit-infested north country.

Miller, Shultz, and Effenburg began their trip by train, but their transportation for the hinterland was the ancient four-geared Dodge truck which "only foreigners would be fools enough to take up there." They shipped the truck on a railroad flatcar as far as Sian in Shensi Province, and then in the car they headed off into the unknown. Their route was over trails which had never before seen a motor vehicle. The old truck climbed mountains, crossed creeks, forded rivers, navigated sand roads and, indeed, negotiated a new obstruction around every bend. The hardy travelers were equipped with jacks, stones, pry-boards, planks, and sufficient gasoline for the round trip. In some places there were no paths, not even for oxcarts, and the Americans had to create their own road as they went. Their only contact with civilization was Harold Shultz's radio, which kept reporting, discouragingly, the rampages of terrorists through the very country in which they were traveling. It could not have been more prophetic.

It took the better part of a week to make the five-hundred-mile trip to Lanchow, and with the ever present threat of bandits, the men were sometimes tempted to turn back. Then a runner brought word from Chinghai that the wife of a Baptist member of the China Inland Mission had been removed, critically ill, to the mission's Sining compound. Giving up all thought of turning back, the men redoubled their efforts to reach her in time.

Somehow they had underestimated the last short lap. The route out of Lanchow continued to be a combination of stones, gravel, sand, irrigation ditches, and rivers. Time and again they were stuck trying to ford streams, and had to jack up the truck or commandeer curious villagers to help pull it out. Every new obstacle brought renewed concern for the ill woman.

With pick and shovel, the travelers leveled many a ditch for crossing, and then built them up again. Added to the hazards of travel were the understandably antagonistic feelings of the people, whose animals would run in fright from the strange behemoth clattering along the road. More than once, horses threw their riders. At the same time, this first motor vehicle to appear in the area was such a curiosity that it was tolerated with a certain awed wonder.

Approaching Chinghai, the men decided on a short cut across a river in order to save time and perhaps a life. They were in the process of driving their truck onto some boards set transversely across the tiny ferry at the river's edge when howling down to the landing came a group of half-drunk bandits, threatening the travelers with guns, knives, and clubs.

Several of the bandits grabbed and held the three men while another one, leveling his gun at the doctor's head, threatened to shoot. Harry Miller knew resistance was useless. He prayed, instead.

Suddenly the bandits ceased their threats to shoot. Shoving the men into the truck, and hopping in themselves, they forced Miller to drive into a nearby enclosure where camels were kept.

"*Puh tsoh!* Don't go!" (As if we could, thought Miller.) "It's no use trying to escape," warned one of the bandits as he closed the gates on the hapless prisoners. The bandit gang retired to one side to discuss the disposition of their prize.

All that night the Americans lay in the back of the truck wondering, as sleepless hour followed sleepless hour, what the next day would bring. Dr. Miller's thoughts were also with the sick woman at Chinghai, and once they strayed back to a much earlier bandit experience when he and Arthur Selmon had been traveling —and the remarkable adventure that had befallen him.

The next morning, without explanation the trio were released— something almost unheard of in China. Providence had saved Harry Miller and his companions from the usual fate of persons captured by bandits. Soon the three were on their way across the river and on to Chinghai. Dr. Miller arrived in time, and as a steward of the Great Physician, his ministrations saved another life.

There was a happy ending for the original errand of the trip, also. The magic of the old Dodge so ingratiated the three men with Governor Ma of the local Province that he made them his personal guests at nearby Sining, his capital close to Lake

Kokonor, and he helped them find the most suitable location for the new mission.

On another, later occasion—October 23, 1938—there appeared on the front page of the *New York Times* this story:

Surgeon Travels Fast

Despite War in China

Hankow, China, Oct. 22—After having been called to Manila to perform a series of goiter operations, Dr. H. W. Miller, noted American surgeon and superintendent of the Seventh-day Adventist Sanitarium in Wuhan, was back in Hankow today, having made a dramatic ten-day round trip between Hankow and the Philippines.

Dr. Miller motored to Hong Kong in a ramshackle 1928-model car, skirting the fringes of the Sino-Japanese fronts in Central China. He caught a steamer at Hong Kong for Manila twenty minutes before the ship's sailing time. Arriving in Manila Dr. Miller spent two days doing twenty-four operations at the Seventh-day Adventist Hospital there.

Then he took a Clipper plane to Hong Kong, where after a day's waiting he boarded a plane for Chunking and flew on to Hankow the same day. . . .

At that time the Japanese were pressing up the Yangtze River toward Hankow—which was to fall to the invaders two days after the *Times* story appeared—so water travel was impossible. The only way for Miller from Hankow to Hong Kong where he would board ship for Manila was the eight-hundred-mile overland route. Dr. Miller's old car was in a precarious state. Alec Eviscovich, the doctor's Russian maintenance man who was himself just recovering from an operation, volunteered to go with Miller on the Hong Kong trip to keep the old Ford pickup, which Miller was using then, in shape. With the doctor at the wheel and Alec patiently tending the car, they made the trip in two days and two nights of steady driving. Just as they reached the Hong Kong border the ancient jalopy coughed its last, its front lights dangling like the head of a tattered rag doll.

Knowing how close the connection would be, Miller had sent

word ahead to the dependable P. L. Williams, mission treasurer in Hong Kong, to have a ticket ready. And Williams was there at the border, waiting in his car to drive Miller to the pier. Black and dusty as the doctor was, and tired from forty-eight hours of continuous driving, he nevertheless quickly changed his clothes and hopped into Williams' car. But there was one more problem. Miller had to have a smallpox vaccination before he could board ship, a matter he had completely forgotten.

"Well, you're a doctor, why don't you make your own certificate," the pier official suggested, tongue in cheek.

"But is that all right?" the cautious Williams asked.

"Well, in this case it seems to me that the main thing is the vaccination," the official replied. "Unless, of course, you want to go to further trouble——"

They certainly were not begging for any red tape at that late hour, and without hesitation Harry Miller inoculated himself and signed his own certificate. On ship, the purser accepted it without question. But on arrival in Manila, the United States health officer was not so easily satisfied.

"Who is this Dr. Miller that signed your certificate?" he inquired.

"I am the Dr. Miller," the surgeon answered.

"Don't you know that you have no right to sign your own health certificate?" he scolded.

As the doctor began in his mild manner to explain the circumstances at Hong Kong, the official pushed him on through:

"Well, you're here. And you're a doctor. So if you had any sense you would get vaccinated, anyway. I don't know what else to do with you."

Two days of goiter operations in Manila increased the Wuhan Sanitarium exchequer by several thousand dollars. That, along with ten thousand dollars raised by some Chinese women in the Philippines who were sympathetic to Madame Chiang Kai-shek, sent the American back to China with continuing gratitude for a Heavenly Father who knows how to care for His own. During his return trip on a Pan-American Clipper, a friend of free China by the name of Alfred Kohlberg introduced himself to Miller. He had heard about the Church's medical work in China, and expressed a strong interest in helping their program.

"Would you mind taking along one thousand ounces of silver?" asked Kohlberg, politely.

"I certainly wouldn't," replied Miller gratefully.

That amounted to another eight hundred dollars under current exchange rates. In the thirties, eight hundred dollars went a long way.

XXI

TO BOW OR NOT TO BOW

THE CHINESE commonly worshiped their ancestors. Had it been merely a matter of patriotism, Dr. Miller and his fellow workers would not have said a word. But bowing by the ancestor-awed people to the picture or image of Sun Yat-sen was a serious problem to practicing Christians. The issue was pointed up sharply in the Church's mission college and academies, which by the mid-thirties spanned the nation.

Following closely the early ideals, the schools combined a thorough academic preparation with a balanced nurture of heart and hand. They served rich and poor alike, and provided work for all. The China Training Institute near Nanking, for example, had established industries in weaving, furniture making, agriculture, and food processing and canning, in addition to the campus kitchen, bakery, and other operations to meet the needs of resident students and staff.

Miller and his colleagues felt that an appreciation of the nobility of labor was generally lacking among the well-to-do of China. Wealthy Chinese were educated to believe that manual work was beneath them.

In China, a manual skill was not considered a matter for schools; it was simply handed down from parent to child. The industrial phase of the Adventist schools was unique in that land. This strange feature provided a peculiar twist when, in the mid-thirties, the Ministry of Education ordered all school personnel and students to bow down to beloved Sun Yat-sen—or the schools must close.

"You and your students will bow daily before the [image or picture of the] founder of our Chinese Republic," the directive stated. It was addressed to all school principals and teachers. "And you will repeat the will [the guiding principles of government] of Sun Yat-sen." To disobey, it was clearly implied, meant disloyalty to the Government. To implement the program, the Government officials proposed to send one of their men to each school to teach the philosophy of the late President Sun. Since the edict left no loophole for any institution under the Ministry of Education, many missions closed their schools. Others bowed, winking at the whole proposition as little more than saluting a flag—a simple, patriotic gesture. But the Adventist schools were the key to the Church's program of service. They were to provide the Christian leaders who eventually would replace the foreign missionaries. "We could not afford this expedient approach," says Dr. Miller.

One day Denton E. Rebok, president of China Training Institute, went to Shanghai and laid the situation in the lap of Dr. Miller, then head of the Church's China Division.

"They are threatening our teachers with fine or imprisonment. This is the showdown," Rebok said with urgency, somewhat impatient with Miller's deliberate handling of the affair.

Miller says now that "Rebok had cause to be uneasy, for word was being passed around that our people were disloyal to China. It would not have taken much to stir up a mob. Rebok was only holding the authorities off while trying to find the best way to close so complex an institution as the industrial school." Harry Miller knew that the teachers at Nanking, both American and Chinese, could not continue in that situation much longer. Some were already seeking assignments elsewhere. If the college teachers left, teachers in the other schools would quickly follow suit.

Miller told Rebok that he would see him later, and then headed for his office as usual. The doctor knew that one of his patients that day would be H. H. Kung, minister of labor and industry. When Kung arrived, Miller listened to his ailments and prescribed treatment. Then he made his appeal.

"Dr. Kung," he said, "we Seventh-day Adventists are loyal to governments all over the world. We conduct schools and pay for their operation, yet we pay the usual Government taxes along with the others who have free schooling for their children. However, the education department of the Nanking Government has imposed upon us some conditions that we as a Christian institution cannot meet. They want to bring non-Christian teachers into our schools where we are training workers to promote spiritual and educational work, and they also want us to bow down to Sun Yat-sen.

"We respect Sun Yat-sen as a great leader, as the Father of this country, and we admire him just as much as we do George Washington. We respect Washington, but we would never think of worshiping him. The education department demands that we shall either close our schools or conform to these regulations. We cannot and will not. Therefore, I suppose we will have to close our schools."

Kung listened intently.

"What a great pity that would be," Miller continued, "since we have established a line of education which China badly needs. We provide opportunity in the college for poor young men and women to come, people who have no other way of getting an education. Here they work their way through school and learn a trade at the same time, so if they can't find employment as teachers or ministers they can be wise farmers, carpenters, metal smiths, or they can work with the Government in technical lines.

All these students receive a double training."

Kung's keen mind had been working rapidly all the while.

"I am a great believer in your principles of education and in what you are trying to do," he told Miller seriously. "I appreciate the situation with which you are confronted, though of course I have no power to change the regulations of the Ministry of Education. But this I can offer you as a suggestion: Why not change the name of your school to 'China Industrial Institute' and continue in your curriculum just as you are? You have two phases to your training. It matters not which you emphasize in your name. You don't need to change your curriculum a particle," Kung re-emphasized. "Just carry on your work as you are. But I will take your institution under my department. Don't worry any more about bowing down to the picture of Sun Yat-sen."

Rebok, who had been waiting at the Miller home, was exceedingly jittery by the time Miller returned from his office.

"What have you decided?" he inquired with strained patience.

Miller laid Kung's plan before him. At first, Rebok was dubious about such an alternative, for he was a thoroughgoing and scholarly Christian gentleman.

"But this comes from a shrewd Government leader who knows what he is doing," Harry Miller pointed out, "and he has the power to make it work."

Rebok returned to the college. With typical efficiency, he had the necessary legal papers in order before the sun had set. Within the week, the local secretary of education, unaware of the agreement with Kung, arrived to investigate the school which was "brazenly turning its back upon China's hero." Rebok met the secretary with all the courtesies and conventions due his rank, but the visitor brushed formalities aside.

"I am here to determine whether or not you will conform to the edict," he growled.

"We are unable to comply, so——"

"Then you will have to close today," interrupted the blustering

Government agent, grim with righteous indignation over a "national affront."

"We have already closed," said the president quietly.

The startled secretary moved to the edge of his chair. Hadn't he seen students and teachers going about their business as usual? Even now he could hear the machinery humming in the college industries, and could look out upon student-farmers tilling the soil nearby.

As if reading his mind, Rebok explained:

"You see, we have many orders for equipment from our industries. Moreover, we can't just turn all of these students away, for the Chinese are very precious to us, and some of them are unspeakably poor."

The secretary began to remonstrate, but Rebok continued without notice of his gesture.

"So we have closed our college as an institution of the Ministry of Education and reopened it as the China Industrial Institute under Dr. Kung, the minister of labor and industry." Rebok tried to tell him as gently as possible, but the bureaucrat gathered together the fragments of his shattered composure as best he could and took off down the road, never to return.

In recalling those events, Dr. Miller adds: "In the weeks following, each of our other schools went through the same routine. Not one had to change a particle of its program, nor did one of them close. Leaders throughout the Orient seemed to grasp the concept of balanced education. During the late thirties in Japan, when mission schools were being closed throughout the nation, Dr. Tsunekichi Mizuno, chief of social and cultural affairs of the Ministry of Education, told our men, 'If you follow your plan [of balanced education] you have no need to worry; if you don't follow it you have no reason to exist.' We understand that in Japan ours was the only Christian mission school to remain open during the Second World War."

In claiming those freedoms for themselves, workers of the

Church had to take care to preserve them for others. They were cautious not to become entangled with the Government. It was for this reason that a short while later they had to turn down an offer, from the Generalissimo and the Central Government, of a fine school and three hundred thousand dollars to begin its operation.

The Generalissimo and Madame Chiang invited Dr. Miller to their mansion at Wuling, where he was treated royally as their house guest. They talked in English because Miller did not readily understand the dialect used by the Generalissimo. Chiang himself does not use English in public, but he does speak it occasionally with friends in his own home. After lunch one day, the Chiangs outlined their plan for Miller and his colleagues to run the school. The American realized the dangers of the proposition. Yet, he was an honored guest, and in the oriental setting he could say little, for frankness is not a Chinese tool.

"But when the three hundred thousand dollars is gone we would have no way to continue," he pointed out weakly.

"Never mind," Madame said soothingly in her excellent English, attempting to quiet his fears. "When that runs out we will set more aside."

It was easy to see that they were determined. He would have to be bolder. So he pointed out that five hundred or a thousand Chinese students who knew little or nothing about Christianity might loathe the school's religious program.

"That is no problem," the Generalissimo replied. "I will sign a proclamation requiring the people to conform to your tenets."

Dr. Miller knew that that would never do. God would not compel the conscience of man. Nor could the Church. "Finally," says Miller in recollection, "I resorted to the old dodge of passing the buck to Washington headquarters, who in the interests of religious liberty and freedom of conscience, tenderly but firmly turned down the gracious offer."

Harry Miller and his colleagues had failed to communicate the truth that Christians are not made by law, that the center of Christianity is Christ, and that He wins only through love. Today, when on China's mainland the fiat of Government seeks to bind the conscience of man, the meaning of Christian freedom stands out more clearly in contrast.

XXII

KIDNAPING THE GENERALISSIMO

In December, 1936, Wuhan Sanitarium—the third hospital made possible by the Young Marshal's gifts—was under construction. Communists in western China were effectively employing to their own ends the growing patriotic spirit, thus causing the Nationalist Government increasing trouble. At the same time, Japanese were pushing down from the north and east. Caught betwixt and between were Generalissimo Chiang Kai-shek's forces. The Generalissimo, fearing the Communists more than the Japanese, ordered Marshal Chang to the northwest to run back the most serious Communist threat.

That was a blow to many of the missionaries because the Young Marshal was a stanch promoter of the Wuhan hospital project, and he would have to leave the Hankow area for Sian. However, Dr. Miller was not altogether sorry that the young ruler had gone north, for Sian was the capital of Shensi Province. Marshal Chang was ruler over all Kansu, the great northwest China territory which included Lanchow, the site of the Sanitarium that had been established from the gift the Young Marshal had handed Miller after the opium cure. What was a temporary discouragement at Hankow brought encouragement to the staff at Lanchow. The Lanchow of ancient times had been at the crossroads of the great desert caravan routes; and in the twentieth century, supplies and equipment were still brought in on camelback and oxcart.

The critical problem in politics was a disagreement between the Young Marshal and the Generalissimo. Chiang Kai-shek was dividing his forces in order to combat both the Communists and the Japanese, but he was throwing the larger segment against the Communists. The Young Marshal, while not a Communist, felt that the Japanese were the more dangerous of the two. He believed that if the Chinese forces were concentrated on the Japanese, then Communist and Nationalist alike would unite against the common foe. In his view, the Generalissimo was dividing the country—a welcome situation for any invader. One can sympathize with the Young Marshal's feelings when one remembers that it was the Japanese who had driven him out of his rich Manchurian territory. In looking back over history one can speculate whether a defeat of Japan at that juncture would have given a different character to the Second World War.

In any event, the Young Marshal was not abounding in enthusiasm to fight his own countrymen, Communist or not. The Generalissimo, becoming impatient with the Young Marshal's delay in carrying out orders, and thinking the young leader had been deceived by some of his underlings, flew with a small bodyguard to Sian to deal with him personally. Administering a sharp tongue lashing to the young commander, the Generalissimo threatened to replace him if he did not carry out a more aggressive campaign against the Communists.

Marshal Chang, already upset at Chiang Kai-shek's strategy, became angry and resentful at the Generalissimo's threats; and in a fit of temper which superseded his normally fine common sense, he permitted a clique of Communist-influenced officers to take the Generalissimo captive. The officers dispatched a small force to the Generalissimo's quarters, shot down his bodyguard, and seized him soon after he had jumped from his window in an effort to escape.

When the news spread that the Generalissimo was captured and in the hands of Marshal Chang, a chill went through all China. It was a national catastrophe. Madame Chiang knew well that there were other generals in Nanking who were quite willing to take over Government affairs. Some of them, in fact, went to her with propositions that they send bombers to Sian to overwhelm the Young Marshal. Madame knew that this would only make a third war front.

"Furthermore," she pointed out, "if you do that you may kill the Generalissimo. Remember, he is a captive, and he injured his spine in that jump."

It was at this crucial moment that Harry Miller was called in by Madame Chiang, who sent word through the mayor of Shanghai. They knew that Miller had worked intimately with the Young Marshal in carrying out his ambitious health program for his people in the north, and they were also well aware of the drug cure of three years earlier. Furthermore, Dr. Miller had been given rather free use of the Marshal's Boeing plane, being flown from place to place by his American pilots, Julius Barr and Royal Leonard. Arrangements were made for a special train to take the surgeon immediately to Nanking to talk the situation over with Madame Chiang and H. H. Kung.

One line of strategy called for Miller to visit the Young Marshal to persuade him to release the Generalissimo. The doctor did not mind the idea of meeting with the young commander. He was grateful for what both Marshal Chang and the Generalissimo had done for his work. But intervening in affairs of state was not the business of a churchman. He suggested that Donald, T. V. Soong, or Madame herself go. Even better, they might all go, for the psychological effect it would have on the Young Marshal. Donald, who had been Marshal Chang's adviser, was counselor to the Generalissimo. Soong was a close friend of both men, and Madame Chiang was a woman of powerful influence. As it turned out, all three did go.

By then the Young Marshal realized that he was in a precarious position; he proved co-operative with the three. They agreed that the Generalissimo would be released and that to save face all around, Marshal Chang would be returned to Nanking, given a perfunctory trial, and released. Unfortunately, it did not work out that way, for the Central Government did not consider this informal arrangement binding.

The first part of the agreement was carried out in good faith. The entire group, including both the Generalissimo and the Marshal, were flown from Sian to Nanking, with Royal Leonard piloting the plane. When they arrived in Nanking, the Generalissimo resumed command and the Central Government imprisoned the Young Marshal without giving him a genuine trial, at the same time commandeering his plane and his pilot. The Marshal has been in protective custody ever since—nearly twenty-four years at this writing. This enforced idleness of Marshal Chang has been a great disappointment to many persons. Miss Elsie Chow, the Marshal's second wife, has been with him throughout, also under Government custody. Their son, Robert Chow, was under the care of an Italian governess in Shanghai at the time of the kidnaping. The Italian lady did not know what to do then, so she went to Miller for help. Under the circumstances, he thought it best for them to go to the Crown Colony of Hong Kong, and he wired P. L. Williams, the mission treasurer there, to make preparations. Williams subsequently took custody of the governess and the boy. Today, Madame Chang, the Marshal's first wife, lives in California, as does Robert Chow also.

Shortly after the kidnaping, the Government confiscated all of the Young Marshal's China holdings.

Dr. Miller and his colleagues had early learned that they must not tie their mission star to the scepter of Government. This was a primary thesis of their Church, which through the years had turned down many millions of dollars of Government monies. Knowing that the missionaries would not accept Government subsidy, the Young Marshal had repeatedly given from his personal funds to ensure the growth of their medical program. Shortly before the Generalissimo was kidnaped, the Young Marshal had given a personal check for twenty thousand dollars for Wuhan Sanitarium. The check had not been cashed when Miller saw the confiscation announcements in the newspapers. He raced to the local branch of the National City Bank of New York, praying as he ran, but weak in faith and fully expecting to have the check turned down. To the doctor's surprise and pleasure, the bank manager had not received formal notification of the confiscation, and he cashed the twenty-thousand-dollar check.

However, they were still short of funds to carry out Marshal Chang's ambitions for medical missions in the Central China area. By the end of the first year of the Young Marshal's imprisonment, the Japanese were pressing down as far as Shanghai. Because of the uncertain political situation, many Chinese had left their homeland. As a result, nearly all of the Church's medical mission work at that time consisted of charity cases, and the hospitals were greatly in need of more money. Although the Young Marshal's holdings in China had been confiscated, Miller knew that Chang had substantial accounts in American banks, and was sure that he would come to their rescue if he knew the situation. But how to get to him? After talking with Marshal Chang's financial adviser, James Elder, Miller was given a letter to deliver to Chang for his signature, to authorize further funds for medical missions.

It was not easy to obtain an interview with a military or a political prisoner in China, and Marshal Chang was both. But sometimes doctors are able to make their way where others are not allowed to go, so Dr. Miller decided to play his medical qualifications to the hilt. To aid in the scheme and to make the difficult situation as innocuous looking as possible, Miller took Marie and their two sons along. The guards at the foot of the prison mountain gave them a pass, on the basis that Miller was the Young Marshal's physician.

They hiked up the mountain to a point near the Marshal's house when a guard commanded them to wait in an old temple nearby. There the doctor was grilled about his purpose in seeing the distinguished prisoner. No explanation availed, however. The sentries, caustic and unfriendly, ordered them to stay at the temple.

Half an hour later, after the guards had cross-questioned the Young Marshal, permission was granted for the interview. Meanwhile, Harry had handed his wife the papers which Elder had provided as a basis for the financial request. As the doctor had anticipated, he was watched every moment of his visit with the Marshal, but Miss Chow received Mrs. Miller and the two sons in another room, relatively unobserved. Then it was that Marie Miller passed the papers to Miss Chow.

The hospitable Marshal invited his guests to dinner. Before dining, the Millers decided to take a stroll in order to provide an opportunity for Miss Chow to give the papers to the Marshal. When they returned, Miss Chow handed Marie the authorization for Elder to spend another twenty thousand dollars on the Hankow project. This gesture of an imprisoned leader was an eloquent commentary on his concern for his people.

XXIII

"MAYOR" MILLER

SHANGHAI WAS OCCUPIED by the Japanese on November 9, 1937. That was no new experience to the residents, however. Some six years before, the city had been attacked by the Japanese just prior to the establishment of the puppet state of Manchukuo in the north. More than once, Dr. Miller had felt the nudge of Japanese bayonets against his back or had faced the business end of a rifle.

One night early in the 1937 occupation, Miller was called from the clinic in the city to the Sanitarium, on an emergency. A curfew was in effect, and soldiers were cutting down stray civilians in the streets. Somehow, the bullets failed to find the doctor as he made his way among dead bodies and climbed to safety over the wall of the hospital compound. However, the perpetual uncertainty of the times finally forced the closing of Shanghai Sanitarium at the end of 1937.

Sadly and laboriously, Harry Miller moved the hub of his activities up the Yangtze River to Hankow. There, on the north side of the river, he established a dispensary-clinic. On the south side, at Wuchang, stood Wuhan Sanitarium and Hospital, already in use though not yet completely built.

Miller planned to feed patients into Wuhan from the Hankow

168

clinic. But where would he find furnishings and staff for such greatly expanded operations? With the closing of Shanghai Sanitarium, the corps of nurses had been disbanded, and the remainder of the foreign medical staff had fled to Manila. Being desperately in need of help, the surgeon braved night travel on a blacked-out train through the war zone to Shanghai. There he searched until he located twenty-five nurses, and in a rented truck he transported them to Hankow. Checking with the Church's school at Chiaotou-tseng near Nanking, he found that there was a large consignment of furniture for Peking Medical College. Since the equipment could not be shipped north as originally planned, Dr. Miller loaded it on a boat and sent it up the river to Hankow, just ahead of China's blockade of the river when stone-filled barges were sunk across the Yangtze.

No sooner were the institutions completed and furnished, in 1938, than the Japanese began a series of air raids. Dr. Miller quickly painted the Stars and Stripes across their roofs. "For more than four hundred attacks we were not molested," he says. "But the mutilated and wounded poured in by truck, boat, and plane. Our ambulance moved out fast every day and night after the air raids and picked up those we could help. The situation became so dangerous that our Chinese doctors left us for Chungking, all except a lady physician, Dr. Constance Jean Wen. She and our faithful nurses worked round the clock to succor the war's victims."

With the Yangtze blocked, the Sanitarium's only supply source was Hong Kong, eight hundred miles away by narrow, twisting mountain roads, some of them under bombardment by Japanese planes. Dr. Miller himself took the truck to the Crown Colony for supplies, equipment, and necessary building materials, leaving Dr. Wen in charge at the Sanitarium. Many times the truck-driver surgeon passed camouflaged areas, with papier-mâché tanks and planes cleverly set up as targets for the Japanese, who thus wasted a great deal of effort and matériel. Miller remembers "the strangely amusing sight" as the Japanese pilots bombed and strafed those models.

But the attacks, by and large, were not humorous. One afternoon Dr. Miller received a telephone call from the Wuchang police chief. "A direct hit on the Military School" were the only words he caught. Allan Boynton, his male nurse and able assistant, went with him in the truck. In Boynton's words: "Heads, arms, legs, and intestines were splattered everywhere. Others, fearfully mangled, were crying for us to put them out of their misery. We placed all but the completely hopeless in the back of the truck and made for the Sanitarium. Dr. Miller saved sixteen that day. Another time we hauled a load all the way from Nanking to Hankow; and then the doctor operated through the night. Eighty of that group can thank him for their lives."

Eventually, on October 25, 1938, the Japanese took over Hankow. A final bombing, a token guerrilla resistance, and all was quiet. Miller's Chinese staff awoke the next morning to the bitter reality of seeing the Rising Sun flag fluttering over the university across the way. The streets of Hankow and Wuchang were littered with bodies of Chinese whom the Japanese soldiers had shot "in case they might cause trouble." The Japanese had already established supply lines with a ferry system across the Yangtze, and they were greatly enlarging the airfield.

One of the bombs made a direct hit on a small dispensary Miller and his helpers had just finished in a crowded, poverty-ridden section of Wuchang. The doctor came upon the disaster accidentally as he was on his way downtown in the ambulance. Stopping, he checked to see if anyone had been hurt. There was not a soul around. Then he heard a faint cry under a pile of bricks and debris, a fallen wall. When he finally removed the rubbish he found one of his clinic workers with a baby in his arms under a table. Except for lime-and-dust-filled eyes, they were none the worse for the experience.

Allan Boynton tells it this way: "Under the circumstances, with all that brick and rubble, and with us under constant bombardment, no one but Dr. Miller would have dug them out. The things he had to lift required superhuman strength, and when he was through his fingers were bleeding from the rough concrete. But he saved two lives, and that was his only thought."

Both Dr. Miller and the Chinese had been expecting the Japanese occupation. Aware of the political immunity and possible safety of the American hospital, about twenty thousand fear-ridden Chinese had crowded into the Sanitarium compound. People without a country, without a government, they carried all their belongings on rickety wheelbarrows or on their backs. Before long they had set up mud stoves and had rigged little cooplike shelters about the hospital grounds. But their food did not last long.

Fortunately, with the co-operation of the International Red Cross, the Sanitarium had stocked rice for just such an emergency. Allan Boynton had hauled five thousand bags, each containing two hundred twenty pounds of rice, across the river, thirty-five sacks to a load, until he had filled the whole first story of the hospital. Harry Miller set up a quota system for food, and forthwith they dubbed him "mayor." He had once been elected city councilman at Takoma Park, Maryland, but he had never thought of governing a little city like this, with twenty thousand refugee mouths to feed.

Moment by moment the doctor's "family" increased. One day the remnants of a Chinese regiment moved in, uniforms, guns, and all. Miller told them to store their guns and ammunition in one of the garages, and they nearly filled it. The next thing the doctor knew, they were discarding their uniforms.

"You can't throw your clothes away!" the American admonished, nevertheless sending them around to the other refugees for civilian togs. They stacked their uniforms with the ammunition. Now the big question was, what to do with all the military gear. The Japanese were on patrol everywhere, for they were taking no chances with lingering Chinese guerrillas.

A day or so later a Japanese cavalry unit was sent to inspect the Sanitarium. To the surprise of the cavalrymen Dr. Miller asked them in, served them hot drinks, Japanese-style, and invited them to look over the hospital. It was filled, of course, with Chinese soldiers, who became alarmed at the sight of the Japanese. But Miller felt that frankness was the best policy, and held nothing back. As it turned out, it was well that he acted as he did. When the Japanese were through inspecting, Miller called them to one side in a gesture of confidence and told them about the group of Chinese soldiers and their weapons.

"The men are greatly distressed," confided the doctor, "and don't know what to do. So we have stacked their things in the garage for you." The Japanese were delighted as well as surprised at the array of rifles and machine guns. Soon they sent a truck for the equipment, and passed the word on to their commander.

Later, several generals appeared to have their pictures taken with the American *oishasan* (doctor) and to present him with a yellow armband, a symbol of neutrality, which made it possible for him to travel freely between the hospital at Wuchang and the clinic in Hankow. Soon the pictures were published in Tokyo papers, with lofty remarks about the American *otomodachi* (friend) of the Japanese high command.

Boynton adds: "And to increase our prosperity, Dr. Miller found an old Swedish outboard motor. He had Alec Eviscovich, our Russian mechanic, tune it up. When we became so tired and distressed that we couldn't stand the pace another minute, the doctor would take us out on the nearby lake for a boat ride. There we sang, prayed, and swapped stories or compared the length of our beards, which we had grown in protest against the invasion. Those boat rides were a real tonic—until another emergency or a bombing raid drove us back inside."

Being seriously short of nurses and qualified help, Miller took a census of the compound "town" and lined up the most capable persons he could find for the hospital. He had to train some as nurses' aides. Others he placed in key positions in the cloistered community as clerks, guards, and laborers. He felt it particularly important to keep everyone busy, idle hands being the Devil's workshop. The Chinese were such inveterate gamblers that within the first week they were developing gaming cliques, something the doctor sought to discourage. On occasion he had to sentence some of the gamblers to confinement—quite an occupation for a missionary!

Keeping twenty thousand Chinese busy was as big a job as feeding them. The task required a certain amount of ingenuity and intrepidity. Allan Boynton boldly drove the Ford truck to the Wuchang Public Works yard, using the gasoline he had stored months earlier on Dr. Miller's instruction. There he and his helpers loaded tons of crushed rock and piles of sewer pipe, and hauled them to the Sanitarium for use in constructing a sorely needed drainage system to keep the large compound dry and healthful for the new "citizens." To crush the rock once it was in place, Boynton had fifty Chinese pull a big steel and concrete roller across the area. Soon they had the smoothest compound anywhere around.

The Japanese guards at the Works yard seemed not to suspect that the Sanitarium did not own the materials from the start, but one day Boynton returned excitedly with word that he had been stopped, taken to the police station, and warned never to return to the yard. No reason was given. Fortunately, by that time his crew had the compound in excellent shape. The job had required just about all the rock and pipe that had been stored at the Works, which the Japanese would otherwise have used in the war.

Nevertheless, secure in his relationships with the Japanese generals, Dr. Miller protested the interference of the military police. In addition, some of the soldiers had gone into the hospital grounds to take oxen, water buffaloes, and other belongings from the Chinese. The Japanese commander unhesitatingly issued a special order that the American Sanitarium was to have "fortunate treatment" and that all soldiers would "respect its bounds as posted by this headquarters." The signs posted said: JAPANESE, KEEP OUT.

Yet, in his complex responsibilities as mayor, police chief, judge, public works engineer, educator, truck driver, and father-confessor, the talents of the physician were not lost. With medicine provided by the ever generous International Red Cross, Harry Miller supervised the treatment of outpatients by the hundreds daily. Even here his police duties did not end. Some unscrupulous "patients" would feign attacks of malaria, diarrhea, or one of a dozen other ailments in order to secure free medicine, which they would sell on the black market. The problem became so serious that the nurses had to insist the medicines be swallowed on the spot. Despite such vicissitudes, the Great Physician appeared ever to be guiding the course of the China Doctor, and the Chinese seemed intuitively to know it.

XXIV

AN OUNCE OF PREVENTION

THE STEADY DETERIORATION of the Chinese situation finally forced missionaries and other foreigners to leave China, and so the years of the Second World War found Harry Miller again living in America. During that period he carried forward a research project which he had pursued, as time had permitted, for several decades.

Through the years of facing the pain-ridden and starving Orient Dr. Miller's greatest concern was preventive medicine and feeding the hungry. "If we can prevent illness, we don't have to cure," he often says. More than fifty years of study and research have convinced him that the soybean, one of man's hardiest, most versatile, and most nutritionally rewarding foods, is a key to feeding the world's poor. The story of that conviction unites all the facets of Miller the man and crowns his life.

The connection between soybean and surgeon has stumped more than one person until he has heard Harry Miller's simple explanation: "Any honest surgeon is concerned as much with prevention as he is with remedy. For many years we have known that the soybean is one of the most complete foods in the world. It might almost be called a miracle food. In the half century after its introduction into United States agriculture the soybean has risen to the number two cash crop in America. Yet, in the Western world, it is usually considered fodder for animals."

Dr. Miller believed it to be his personal responsibility to dispel this ignorance and to make the food known.

Out of primitive oriental beginnings he turned this "animal food" into human nourishment which today is saving the lives of thousands of babies and is making more comfortable the lives of countless adults. His ingenious development of a palatable milk from the lowly soybean seems destined to bring a new lease on life to millions, of all ages, throughout the world, and he considers this only one step along a freeway of possibilities.

His achievements in developing milk from the soybean are no health faddist's concoction. This milk appears to be the answer to the prayers of many thousand allergy patients and aged people who are unable to drink dairy milk. Mothers who have heretofore lost their babies through inability of these children to take milk from the breast—or the dairy—are turning more and more to this new food. Some physicians call it the "miracle milk." To avoid controversy with dairymen it is officially called Soyalac.

It was at the Lockwoods in Kobe, on his first trip to the Orient, that Harry Miller's curiosity was stirred by the soybean curd, a common oriental food. He determined to find how this tofu was processed. His work in the Far East gave him ample opportunity. As the years passed he became so conversant with the soybean that he was honored with gold medals by nutritionists and medical men the world around. When the vegetarian dining room of Shanghai Sanitarium became crowded with the elite of the nation, its most important and versatile food was the soybean.

In his early China years one problem bore heavily on the doctor. Chinese mothers were losing thousands of babies every year because of allergies and nutritional deficiencies. Often the weak Chinese mother had little or no breast milk to offer her child, and there were not enough wet nurses. In America, animal milk was an answer to such a situation, but relatively few Chinese knew the benefits of a milk cow. The helpless feeling that this problem generated in Harry Miller was an unusual experience for him. He determined to find a food for the babies.

In Shanghai one day Miller watched a local tofu maker grind soaked soybeans in his stone mill. "I lingered to watch the old man strain and cook the white liquid formed from water and the bean," says the doctor. "As I gazed on the boiling soup I was surprised to see a scum form on top, much like that of cow's milk, only a good deal tougher. It was so strong, in fact, that the man hung it up to dry and later used it to wrap up combinations of cooked food in little balls—a delicacy for the Chinese."

After the next step, Harry asked a question. The operator had sprinkled some calcium sulphate (plaster of Paris) in the liquid to coagulate it, and had then made it into soy "cheese"—the same tofu Harry had tasted in Kobe years before.

"But why don't you use the milk as is?" he asked. As a surgeon, he didn't relish the idea of mixing his food with the makings of plaster casts.

"Try it and see." The half-closed eyes of the old Chinese twinkled as he spoke.

Try it Harry did. An acute stomach-ache, overpowering gas pains, and diarrhea soon told him why. His every violent belch brought back the raw, bitter, bean taste to remind him of his folly. Yes, the Chinese seemed to have a reason for everything. In the days that followed, Harry Miller's questioning mind could not shake his dream of the healing potentialities in that high-protein bean milk. There must be a way to process the bean, he insisted, "so that all, even babies, can have its food."

Thus it was that the surgeon-scientist took on the challenge. His curiosity gave birth to countless studies. He compared the soy liquid with cow's and goat's milk and with milk from the human breast. He found the soy richer in protein, lower in fat, and with less carbohydrates. He knew the soybean to be the world's greatest source of vegetable oil, but he discovered that it contained twice as much protein as oil. He noted, on the other hand, its contrast with other vegetable protein and oil foods—beans, wheat, and corn—which are high in carbohydrates.

As Harry Miller followed his determined way toward the development of an appetizing and healthful soy milk, he found that the road of the pioneer is often a discouraging obstacle course. Like a Paul Bunyan stepping from mountain to mountain, he plodded patiently from problem to problem over the years— not always sure of his method but ever certain of his goal. "Our first and most formidable barriers were the bitterness and indigestibility of the soybean liquid," says Dr. Miller. "Generous amounts of sugar did little either to turn the taste or to enhance the healthful qualities of the drink. Although early experiments showed that babies do not have adult taste prejudices, their rebellion was frequently demonstrated through loose stools."

Preservation of the milk was another worry in the Orient. At the time it seemed unlikely that "soy-milk dairies" would be able to provide a fresh delivery daily. But what proved to be the most difficult obstruction was the pampered American taste. Any soy milk, in order to enjoy reasonable acceptance in the Western world, must compare favorably to the flavor of animal milk.

Miller's early attempts to milk the soybean followed a set pattern: soak the beans; grind them in a stone mill, with a stream of water running through them; tediously filter the milky solution through a cotton cloth, as was done in the backwoods American dairy at the turn of the century; finally, boil the liquid and then add sugar and flavoring in an effort to cover the bitterness of the bean. But, alas, even the strongest essences were no more effective than adding vanilla to castor oil. The obnoxious bean taste stubbornly remained.

At first Dr. Miller was worried about the extensive processing of the soybean. Many foods, including animal proteins, become increasingly indigestible as they are processed. But, as is the case with most vegetable protein, the opposite proved to be true of the soybean.

While experimenting with the manufacture of a palatable soy milk, Miller was also seeking to produce it as a colloidal solution, i.e., a solution in which very fine particles are suspended in liquid so that it does not separate. If human and animal milk are colloidal and will hold a suspension of emulsified oil, why not soy milk, he reasoned. By that time he had come to the conclusion that the bitter taste of soy milk resulted from the natural oils of the bean. The problem was to eliminate the natural oils and then to combine the necessary amount of other vegetable oils with the colloidal milk.

In the early nineteen-thirties, while returning to the United States on furlough, Miller discovered that the milk served on board ship did not have the usual rancid taste. Seeking out the steward, he asked why.

"Come down and see," the officer replied, beckoning Miller to the galley. "We don't carry whole milk. We dissolve skim-milk powder in hot water, add melted sweet butter, and run it through this thing." He rapped his knuckle on a small homogenizer installed near the cold room. "The result is like fresh whole milk. And if we want cream we just add more butter."

Harry Miller learned a lot in a moment: "I knew then that I could add soy oil to soy liquid and have fresh-tasting soy milk. This might be part of the answer, not only for taste, but also to the problem of preserving the milk, especially if I could spray-dry our liquid soy."

Quickly he wrote letters to manufacturers around the world, and on his return to Shanghai his first milk plant began to take shape: a Japanese bean grinder, an American extractor for straining the fiber from the slurry, a Chinese stove for boiling the milk, and a new American homogenizer. Later, he added a small spray drier to make it into powder.

The process proved so effective that in that soy milk—unlike other soy milks—not even a fiber was left to clog a baby's nipple. Soon he had an improved soy milk for the babies, patients, and staff at Shanghai Sanitarium. The Chinese, unfamiliar with cow's milk, did not object to the taste. For them, the bitterness problem was virtually whipped!

Harry Miller's mounting enthusiasm met only with heightened impatience and ridicule from some of his American friends. Says one friend: "Wherever he went he was always mixing concoctions and stewing around, even in the hinterlands of Manchuria." Some accused him of wasting valuable time. Others thought it "undignified for a talented surgeon to be always playing around with beans." Even his brother Clarence at first joined the opposition, although he later became one of the doctor's loyal supporters. American critics did not daunt Miller, however. He had early become inured to rough treatment from many sources and had learned that not all problems can be met head on.

He sought out men who shared his goals. One of these was Dr. J. A. LaClerc, at the time chief chemist of the United States Department of Agriculture, who strongly encouraged him. Dr. LaClerc wrote that "soy milk contains all the amino-acids known to be essential for growth . . . [is] rich in iron . . . compares very favorably with animal milk as to its nutritional and biologic values. Soya milk has this further advantage that it does not expose the user to disease-producing germs."

This encouraged the surgeon, who closed his ears to ridicule and set about conquering what he hoped would be his last major obstacle—taste. Even though the soy bitterness was almost gone, he knew that for any large-scale success with Americans and other Westerners he would have to get rid of the lingering bean flavor that dogged him like the bossy-cow flavor of milk in his old dairy days.

After his regular surgery schedule one day, on a hunch he decided to cook some soy milk in the Shanghai Sanitarium kitchen steam cooker, running the steam directly into the milk. The staff and patients quickly noted both improved flavor and greater digestibility, for the aeration further reduced the milk's gas-forming potential. With this method he could eliminate nearly all of the original oil from the liquid and reconstitute it in any amount he wanted. Like the ship's steward, he even made "cream" by adding more soy or peanut oil.

He began anew his experiments in feeding it to babies, and was overjoyed to find the onetime aftereffects almost gone. The soy milk was proving a satisfactory alternative for mother's milk. He *would* save those babies! There followed extensive tests on patients with stomach trouble, with elderly people, and with persons afflicted by sprue. This was a gratifying experience in itself, in view of Maude's death years before, and the suffering sprue had caused him.

With the prospect of success within reach, he began to revise and redefine his goals: (1) the bean taste must go; (2) the milk must be capable of being made into a formula containing specific quantities of fat, sugar, protein, minerals, and vitamins; (3) a way must be found to spray-dry the liquid into a powder that could be completely reliquefied; (4) it must be able to be preserved as a liquid or as a powder; (5) it must remain a colloid liquid; (6) it must be bacteria-free; (7) its price must be within the reach of all.

During this period, when he was making frequent trips to the Philippines to perform goiter operations, Miller toured the Philippine Refining Company, where the stench of drying copra recalled to him his visits to the old Chicago slaughterhouses; but his keen sense of smell noted that the finished product, a sweet-flavored, solid (hydrogenated) coconut oil, had none of the dead-animal smell.

The Filipinos processed out the odor, Miller learned, by steam distillation. His curiosity was awakened further when he heard of a nearby produce company that specialized in refining stale and rancid butter. Their product tasted as fresh as that from his mother's churn. Flash pasteurization was the secret. It effectively killed bacteria.

In China, the doctor together with his older son, Harry Willis, Jr., who was assisting his father part time in research on the soybean, worked out both these methods for processing the milk. The result was a readily digestible and gas-free soy milk, notable for its lack of bean flavor. He expanded his experiments with infants and children, and in 1936 his findings were published in the staid *Chinese Medical Journal*. It was officially noted for the first time that babies could be nourished from birth fully as well with soy milk as with animal milk.

Paul Bunyan had taken a long stride indeed. Those victories led to the establishment of a soybean milk plant on Pting Liang Road in Shanghai, not far from Dr. Miller's Shanghai clinic. There the doctor worked with his production manager, Harry, Jr., who later was to become a consultant for the United Nations Food and Agricultural Organization.

From the outset, however, the customers in areas without refrigeration were plagued by spoilage. After studying the American techniques for keeping milk drinks, Harry Miller and his helpers installed in-bottle sterilization equipment, and began deliveries anew. The milk kept indefinitely until uncapped.

Malt and chocolate flavors were provided for the sophisticated taste. A special yogurtlike milk was praised by many; even non-Chinese began to drink it. Soon Miller was producing the ultimate —a primitive "soy ice cream." The price of the milk competed easily with that of cow and goat milk.

In the late thirties, Japan was invading China. Within months after the soy-milk business began booming, a Japanese bomb blew up the Shanghai plant. Scientist Miller's plans collapsed around him. But the war could not take away his experience unless it took his life.

The doughty surgeon returned to the United States, convinced that soy milk was destined for world-wide acceptance. He went at the task with typical enthusiasm, and soon formed the International Nutrition Laboratory in Mount Vernon, Ohio, the town where he had gone to school as a boy. But as is usually the case with inventors, not all the world was as convinced as Harry Miller.

However, Ohio was a great agricultural state known for its soybean crop. Ohio State University had taken especial interest in the development of varieties of the bean, and was a first-rate source of information for Dr. Miller. Furthermore, although Mount Vernon was not on a railroad line, it did lie on a truck route.

Working with his son, Harry, Jr., Dr. Miller began his search for a suitable location for a soy-milk production plant. To his happy surprise he found a one-hundred-forty-acre farm within a mile of his alma mater, Mount Vernon Academy. The people from whom he purchased it had been drilling hopefully but unsuccessfully for natural gas, and their failure led them to part with the land "for a song."

Before making his purchase, Dr. Miller had to be sure about water. Fortunately, the acreage contained many fine springs, just what he needed for a soybean processing plant where a substantial supply of good water is an absolute necessity. Moving into the one usable house on the property, he set up shop, with his first production plant fitting nicely into the garage.

With little more than the few coins in his pocket Miller boldly made plans for a sixty-by-one-hundred-thirty-foot building, which he planned to enlarge later with the addition of a second story. He had laid the foundation before he knew where he would find the materials to finish the building, but again Providence smiled on him: the Mount Vernon High School building had recently been torn down, and all the old bricks could be purchased for fifty dollars. Day after day Dr. Miller and his son—with whatever help they could find—spent their time at the school site cleaning mortar from the aged bricks and hauling them in their Ford truck—the combination family wagon and limousine.

Dr. Miller at the wheel of the old Ford became a familiar sight: a distinguished surgeon known the world over, meeting his regular appointments in a ton-and-a-half truck. Whether going to church, visiting on weekends, meeting professional appointments, or hauling bricks, it was the only conveyance he had. Such economy measures were absolutely necessary, he felt, if the soybean venture were to be a success.

Day after day his willing hands moved from scalpel and suture to bricks and mortar, belying the common impression that a surgeon's fingers must never endure rough work. He recruited his other son and his brother. A preacher helped him lay the brick. Miller dug ditches, mixed mortar, carried brick, and did everything he could to keep down the cost of building.

At one time he was faced with the necessity of employing an extra boiler man. Clad in his overalls, Miller went to Columbus to take the examination for a boiler license. As with the examinations for his medical licenses, he passed without question, to the consternation of his employees and of the examining board, whose members had identified him the moment they saw his name.

As time passed, Miller and his helpers had to face, in Miller's own words, "a truth that we really knew all along, namely, that the United States is basically a dairy country, and as long as there are goats and cows around, people will wonder why we milk a soybean. So for the time being we set about using our beans in developing meat substitutes for vegetarian palates. We never quite liked the idea of calling them meat substitutes, however, for I have always felt that meat was given man only temporarily after the Deluge as a substitute for fruits, vegetables, grains, and nuts."

Miller developed "vegeburgers," vegetable "wieners," and soy cheese, and before long he had a line of products that was making money. However, they did not provide sufficient money for his soy-milk ambitions. He continued his medical and surgical practice, this time as medical director of the Mount Vernon Hospital, putting every spare penny into the soybean business. Soon he was able to purchase a large spray drier to turn liquid milk into powder. Next came ice cream mixes and other variations of the formula milk which by then had been named Soyalac.

But what to do with all the powdered milk in dairyland America? Again the doctor turned to the Orient. For the two years between 1939 and the outbreak of the Second World War in 1941, Filipino and Chinese markets absorbed all he could manufacture. The bombing of Pearl Harbor, with the subsequent curtailment of transportation to Asia, put an end to this. Potentially it meant ruin for the fledgling business. Then it was that Harry Miller, his back against the wall but never one to admit defeat, actively promoted in the United States a formula he had long before developed in China—an allergy-free baby food which would not clog a nipple. Not only were many mothers unwilling or unable to feed their babies, but many of the little ones were allergic to their own mother's milk. Often cow's milk only made matters worse. The allergies and other afflictions showed up in various ways including atopic dermatitis, asthma, diarrhea, projectile vomiting, nervous irritability, and other baffling problems.

Hundreds of infants were being sacrificed. After several physicians agreed to try soy milk on sick babies, and observed that the vegetable protein did not develop the allergies found in the animal products, the local market increased.

By then, Miller had learned that the alkaline nature of his Soyalac could also do things for adults which acid-prone animal milk could not do. Not only was Soyalac free from allergy-producing elements, but it helped diabetics, arthritics, ulcer and colitis patients, and those with atherosclerosis. It did not increase the blood cholesterol, and it proved to be an excellent postoperative food for abdominal-surgery patients. The formula for adults, which varied from that for babies, was dubbed Soyagen. Both Soyagen and Soyalac have biological properties and chemical behavior similar to breast milk.

Although the enthusiasm of the few who tried soy milk was encouraging, the sales resistance of the medical profession as a whole was another mountain in the doctor's path.

"Just take a few samples and try it," Miller encouraged fellow doctors as he visited from hospital to hospital and office to office. He became very familiar with the vicissitudes of a traveling salesman.

The doctors asked him hard questions: "What research evidence do you have on this milk?" "How do we know that it is safe to use?" The physicians, accustomed to well-documented publications, were often skeptical of the aging medico.

At first, Miller was stymied; then one day he made his sales talk to a friendly but scientifically inclined physician who suggested that a sample of the milk be submitted to the American Medical Association. Miller thought it an excellent idea and at once started on the long road of controlled experimentation to prove the value of both Soyalac and Soyagen. Dr. Earl Baxter, imaginative researcher and professor of pediatrics at Ohio State University, agreed to carry on some comparative studies, feeding to one group of babies cow's milk and to the other soy milk.

Harry Miller knew, however, that there should be more than one study. Realizing that his own published experiments would not carry much weight with the American Medical Association, he sought out other unbiased research agencies and scientists. Among them was Dr. Choei Ishibashi in Tokyo, later president of the Japan Medical Society.

The Japanese, like the Americans, did a meticulous research job, checking blood, measurements, growth records, and other essential data on their patients over a period of many months. Comparisons between the soy-fed babies and those fed with animal milk were carefully tabulated. Those tabulations Miller submitted to the Council on Food and Nutrition of the American Medical Association, made up of some of the most discriminating foods and nutrition scientists in the nation. The Council examined the milk and the claims for it, guardedly scanned the well-documented research reports, and finally awarded their seal of approval. That was a great day for Harry Miller.

The seal of the American Medical Association in itself carried a potent promotional punch. It stimulated the interest of thousands of physicians in the new food. But the secretary of the American Medical Association had a word of caution:

"Don't you think your claims are a little strong?" he asked Miller with more certainty than query.

"No, I don't think so," Miller replied with equal certainty, but in a tone of voice which let the secretary know that he was open to further suggestion.

"You must recognize that cow's milk is the main food supply for babies in America," the secretary reminded him.

This Harry Miller readily acknowledged.

"Wouldn't it be better," the official offered tactfully, "to say that soy milk can take care of those babies who do not thrive on cow's milk?"

"We will be happy to do that," the surgeon agreed, and both of them had a good laugh.

"Of course," the secretary rejoined, "if you can take care of babies that cow's milk does not take care of, there is no reason why you cannot take care of other babies that cow's milk does agree with, too."

Actually, with that word the secretary of the American Medical Association had given him more encouragement than had anyone else. "And," Dr. Miller recalls, "he had shown me a technique of sales diplomacy, besides. Since then we have carefully avoided unfriendly comparisons with cow's milk."

Much more trying was Harry Miller's examination by the United States Patent Office. Looking like a patent-medicine man with his liquid and powder samples, he was subjected to the most intensive grilling he had ever experienced. But the patent officers, finally admitting that his was the first truly nonbitter soy milk, awarded the patent. To Miller's delight, Patent 2078962 also recognized his achievement of his other major goals for soy milk: digestibility, preservability, and capability of being made into any given formula.

This success spurred him on to even greater research. He became so deeply engrossed in his studies that he found the production program a distraction. Soon he sold his Mount Vernon plant to Loma Linda Food Company of Arlington, California. Then, characteristically, he turned around and used much of the money from that sale to help establish the International Nutrition Research Foundation, also at Arlington.

Before long, Soyalac was in demand at prescription pharmacies across the nation. Later, the Loma Linda Food Company began distribution of Soyagen in favorite flavors at food stores. Overseas milk plants were licensed by Miller, first in Manila and Hong Kong and then in other countries around the world.

Today, Harry Miller's International Nutrition Research Foundation fosters numerous studies, some of them in co-operation with major foundations. They are developing "cholesterol-free" cheeses, salad oils, spreads, and ice cream mixes. They are running infant-feeding experiments under the joint sponsorship of the International Nutrition Research Foundation and the Rockefeller Foundation. Dr. Paul Gyorgy, director of pediatrics at Philadelphia General Hospital, and a leading Rockefeller researcher, lauds Harry Miller, "who almost singlehanded popularized 'soya milk' as a substitute for infant feeding."

In the last few years the United Nations also has taken an increased interest in Dr. Miller's research. Its World Health Organization, working with UNICEF and the Food and Agricultural Organization, has launched programs of soy-milk production along the lines of FAO's pilot plant in Djakarta, Indonesia.

Out of long and deep experience, Dr. Miller some years ago made a prophecy already substantiated by leading scientists: "As the world shrinks and the population grows, there will probably be a shortage of edible protein. Few then will be able to afford the luxury of meat proteins or animal milk—both secondhand foods. Insect-resisting soybeans can be substituted for less productive crops, for soybeans not only grow in practically any soil and climate but produce considerably more food per acre than almost any other vegetable or grain. Then disease-free soy milk will become a staple of the adult diet as well as of the diet of the infant."

As always happens with a successful discovery, a number of manufacturers have joined the soy-milk parade. This does not disturb the China Doctor. "Just so the people get the milk," says Harry Miller, "I do not worry how." Nor does he want to hurt the dairyman. "We are planning for important developments," he points out. "Actually, our soybean research is helping the dairy farmer. After all, what would the cows do without soy meal? Furthermore, we take up where cow's milk leaves off."

Uppermost in Harry Miller's mind are the starving babies of the Orient. His heart is grieved when he thinks of the hunger of nutritionally weakened mothers whose empty breasts sag more from exhaustion than from the suckling of their little ones. Therefore, he is perfecting a small soy-milk processing machine which will be within the financial reach of village tofu makers. Dr. Miller is confident that this device, already backed by several nations, will soon be used throughout the milk-starved areas of the world. Judging from his past achievements, his confidence is justified.

XXV

SHANGHAI AGAIN

HARRY MILLER's hound-tooth-clean record of refusing to take sides in Chinese affairs stood him in particularly good stead in 1949 when the Communists completed their China coup. At that time, Dr. Miller, still making his home in America, was on a business trip to Hong Kong, arranging for the development of a soybean milk factory, when he was asked to take over Shanghai Sanitarium again. Miller was then seventy years old. The American doctors who had been in Shanghai accepted the advice of their consul general and had left.

Dr. Miller's presence in China would be an embarrassment to no one. He knew, and was known by, both Communists and Nationalists. Also, he did want to ensure the future of the hospitals and clinics which had been his "babies" for nearly fifty years. Nevertheless, there was one big stumbling-block. Marie Miller was ill in the Mount Vernon, Ohio, hospital—critically ill, the doctor found, when he arrived back in the United States.

Much as he wanted to return to China, he could not go without Marie. She had stood by him for forty years. They prayed, believing that if God really wanted them to go, He would open the way—and He did. Marie rallied. In a few days she was up and around, and though her health was yet delicate, she felt she could do as well in China as in America.

By then they had received word that the Communists had taken Nanking and were approaching Shanghai, the last northern bastion of the Nationalist forces. The United States Department of State had restricted the issuance of passports, but the Millers already had their American passports as well as their visas from the Nationalist Government of China, which was all that was necessary. It was important only that they arrive before the Nationalists were entirely gone. Pan American Airways quickly worked out the details, as they had done for Dr. Miller a score of times before, and soon the Millers were on their way to the first stop, Hawaii. There the immigration authorities looked at them strangely.

"Why on earth do you want to go to China?" asked an astonished officer.

"Because I am responsible for some hospitals there," the doctor replied.

"But certainly you aren't going to take your wife?" another insisted.

"Yes, we have lived together for forty years, and she still loves me," Harry told them.

They shook their heads.

"Our instructions are that no one goes to Shanghai unless given special clearance."

"Here are our passports and visas," Miller told them with a bold façade while breathing a prayer. A moment later the officials opened the gate and let them board the plane.

At Tokyo the news was no better. Shanghai was being fortified in the hope that the Generalissimo, with his many American gunboats, aircraft, and mechanized units, could stave off the Communists, but Pan American officials were pessimistic.

"We will make our hop to Hong Kong," the Tokyo manager told the Millers, "but it looks as though our Shanghai stop is out."

"But we *have* to get to Shanghai," Miller said. "I'm certain things will open up for us to land there."

The manager smiled sympathetically.

"We'll put you up in the Imperial Hotel for the night," he offered. "Then we'll see how things are in the morning."

The next morning Miller received word that the pilots would try Shanghai.

"Good old Pan Am," Harry said, passing the news to Marie. Pan American had carried him faithfully from the era of its earliest "Clippers," years before. Harry and Marie were soon off, but as they neared Shanghai their captain, F. L. Rodman, could detect no radio responses from the airport.

"As far as I know the Commies haven't taken over yet," he informed the Millers, "although they are besieging the city. The airfield is pockmarked, and there is considerable doubt whether we should land."

"I am sure you can," Dr. Miller encouraged him with more bravado than faith. He knew there were only three passengers for Shanghai: Marie, an agent for the Chase National Bank, and himself. "Just drop us off," he pleaded. "That's all we want."

"If we can land we'll let you off," the captain promised. "Otherwise, we'll have to go on to Hong Kong."

Rodman circled round and round the airport waiting for a signal to land; but none came. He continued to circle. Harry and Marie believed that if it were God's will, they would land. After circling for a few minutes more the pilot decided to make a try.

"Make your preparations to jump off quickly," he instructed. "We are not killing the motors." He brought the big craft down gently.

In describing that scene, Miller says: "In a few moments we were out of the plane, its propellers still turning. The airport officials were as surprised as little kids to see us leave that plane. Before they could get out to us, the DC-4 was off for Hong Kong." All that the Millers had with them for their stay in China were the clothes on their backs and the contents of their bags.

Dr. Miller continues: "Marie braved gunfire and moved with me to the Sanitarium on the outskirts of the besieged city. But unfortunately, in their retreat the Nationalists hit the hospital with a number of cannon shells, and it was a real mess. Between attacks, we had to move all equipment possible into the city clinic.

"After the Communists took over, we cleaned and patched up the Sanitarium as best we could, and moved the equipment back. The most serious damage was to our American-made elevator. We called in agents for the manufacturer and also a Chinese elevator man to estimate costs of repair." The local man, who had worked on similar equipment before, submitted a modest bid. But the American firm's price was six times as high.

"We just don't have that kind of money," Miller told the American agent.

"No one else can do the job right," he replied with finality.

"There simply isn't enough money," the missionary repeated.

"You'll be sorry," was the answer, expressing the average American's indifference to the industrial and mechanical know-how of the oriental. But Harry Miller had confidence in the Chinese, and in a few days the Chinese mechanic had the elevator in excellent working order.

When Shanghai fell to the Communists on May 25, 1949, the Millers were cut off from everything and everybody outside of China. Even the United States consul could not help them, although eventually they did get a few telephone calls through to Hong Kong. The conquerors were friendly, however. The Millers found that their principal problems resulted from the Communists' puzzling new ways of doing business. There were the banks, for example.

Virtually all of the regular bankers had fled to Hong Kong. Communist bankers took over, their first move being to issue new currency. It soon developed that although they might be able to issue currency, they had little idea what to do with it once it was in circulation. For instance, several Communist-run banks accepted money from depositors, carefully counted and receipted it, and then placed each deposit in an individual sack for storage in a vault. Soon the vaults were piled high with the small bags. It was not until other banks, in the hands of more experienced personnel, investigated to discover why these particular banks had no money available for their commitments that this novel banking procedure was brought to light.

Within a few weeks the Sanitarium was repaired, staffed, and filled with patients. Everything went well for a number of months despite the Millers' isolation and the fact that they were, from one point of view, enemy aliens. Then came the sad word from the United States consulate that they must leave. The S.S. *General Gordon* was being sent to evacuate all Americans to Hong Kong. To the Millers, this was disappointing news; but, as United States citizens, they had no recourse.

They began the weary routine necessary to departing the country. "We had left foreign countries many times, but never under circumstances like those," says Harry Miller. "Crowds of foreigners were in line at the Communist offices for exit visas. Like the Belgian ticket agents of the early years, they sharply limited their hours for business. We went back early day after day to wait in line. Marie became ill, but she had to wait with the rest of us, for each one had to speak for himself. Then we had to pay the newspapers to print notices of intention to leave Shanghai, in the event we owed any bills or there were other reasons why we should not leave."

Like a fantastic merry-go-round the line-up was repeated, many times in many places for many things: fingerprints, intelligence checks, money exchange, customs inspection, stamping of numerous cards and documents. The waiting lines seemed to dwindle more by attrition than by orderly bureaucracy. "I have often watched housewives waiting their turn in supermarket or department store, impatient or torn with frustration," says the surgeon in wry humor. "I have listened as they lightly tossed off a note of exasperation, 'Will I *ever* get out of here?' and I have had to smile, for we used those same words. Only to us it was a stark question of life or death. And to this day, I wonder how our crowd on the *Gordon* ever made that obstacle course!"

At Hong Kong, W. H. Branson, president of the China Division, met the Millers with the request that the doctor accompany him on a quick trip to Chungking in the west, where the Church had another hospital and headquarters. The Communists were not far away, and Branson wanted to see the situation at first hand. There they met the doctor's old friend, Chang Chuen, formerly China's premier and at that time governor of Szechwan Province.

"Don't linger here," the governor warned sadly. "We have no hope." The reality of those despairing words was impressed upon the Americans a few hours later when they were on their way back to Hong Kong. They asked to stop at Canton. But, as the plane lowered its gear for a landing, the pilot was given a signal not to stop. Canton was already occupied by the Communist army. The pilot sped up his motors and flew on.

XXVI

CHINA'S GREATEST HONOR

MARIE MILLER never had been hardy. The strain of the life of a busy surgeon's wife kept her frail body taxed to the limit, and sometimes beyond. She often accompanied her husband on his travels, she was always the busy hostess and mother, and her health suffered. Many times during Harry's extended trips she had to be both mother and father to their four children. Soon after the Millers' evacuation from China to the United States in 1950, Marie became seriously ill and required constant care.

Except for one emergency trip to the Orient for a round of thyroid surgery, Dr. Miller cared for her every night, never knowing what the next hour would bring. Although he studied every known therapy for her illness and had for her the moment-by-moment concern growing out of more than forty years of companionship, Marie went steadily down.

On October 9, 1950, Harry Miller was left alone once again.

Then seventy-one, the doctor turned more and more away from surgery to study and research in a vain effort to shake off a depressing mantle of loneliness. His heart urged him to work harder than ever to find the means to prevent disease and the heartaches that follow in its train. For more than three years he worked intensively on food research, concentrating for the most part on the soybean. Yet the loneliness of those years did not abate.

In 1953, while combining soybean business with surgery on a Far Eastern tour, Dr. Miller was again challenged by the Orient's needs. The challenge came from Ezra Longway, a friend from old China days.

"Dr. Miller, we need a hospital in Formosa," Longway said one day. "The medical work is the right arm of the Church."

"What do you have in mind?" Miller queried.

"I'd like to see you come here and start a Sanitarium like the one we had in Shanghai," he answered.

"At my age?" Harry Miller asked in astonishment, for he knew that normal retirement policies sent missionaries home by age sixty-five. He was nearly a decade past that mark.

"Who else?" Longway replied. "You are still able-bodied, and what's more, you know the language. Nobody in the Orient knows as much about starting hospitals as you do."

The challenge was too dear to his heart for Harry Miller to be able to forget it. Yet, the more he considered it the less he wanted to undertake the task alone. He kept thinking of a lovely girl—a schoolteacher—he knew in Mount Vernon, Ohio. Her name was Mary Elizabeth Greer.

With thoughts of attractive, sweet-singing Mary in his mind, Harry Miller returned to America. The big question was: Would she marry him, some forty years her senior? His fears were stilled by Mary's happy response, "Some men are fossilized at twenty-five. Others are young in heart at a hundred."

She knew that she was marrying adventure. ("Your wildest imagination could never approach the real adventure of our life," Mary wrote the author later on.) As soon as passports were in hand, the newlyweds were off from New York for London, Paris, Beirut, Damascus, Karachi, Calcutta, the island of Ceylon, Bangkok, Singapore, and Hong Kong.

Mary recalls: "Within five minutes after we arrived in the Crown Colony [Hong Kong] we were told there was an emergency in our hospital at Penang, Malaya. One doctor was sick and the other would be if he did not have a long overdue rest. It was plain to me that Harry was needed, especially since he was the only available surgeon who had British qualifications. Besides, the hospital buildings at Formosa were not yet completed, and he could be released for a month or so. We decided that he should return south alone while I remained at Hong Kong for Chinese language study." This meant a break in their honeymoon. "But Chinese is best studied without distractions, anyway," Mary adds with a twinkle.

Dr. Miller kept in touch with Formosa developments by correspondence. Yet, even with all the pleasantness of the Penang staff, he was glad a month later to pick up Mary and make his way to Taipei, Formosa. Before leaving the United States he had purchased quantities of hospital equipment from army surplus. These were already on their way to the island, and gave him reason for concern. "The Formosan customs and commodities laws, like those of most countries," he notes, "are subject to considerable interpretation. If the customs officers want to be strict they can and will levy maximum charges at the drop of a trunk lid. If they are convinced that you are doing something for the Chinese people they are often as indulgent and liberal as American parents." Fortunately, most of the officials of the customs and postal services and other Government agencies had been Miller's patients at one time or another. He knew that if he were there when the things arrived, he would be saved many precious dollars. And so it turned out.

Meanwhile, he made arrangements for necessary additions to the staff of the Formosa hospital. There was Chief Nurse Elizabeth Redelstein who had for years been personal nurse to Madame Chiang Kai-shek, and Muriel Howe, a capable Australian nurse educator in Shanghai Sanitarium, who had headed their nursing school. He managed also to secure an able American doctor, Edwin Brooks, who had married Leatha Coulston, former head American nurse from Shanghai Sanitarium.

Taiwan Sanitarium, as it was named, was ideally located a scant mile from the Taipei airport on the prominent Chiang Kai-shek traffic circle. The opening ceremonies brought out a number of Formosan leaders, including Madame Chiang herself. Foreign dignitaries, among them America's Ambassador Karl L. Rankin, filled the flag-draped platform.

But what made the occasion particularly unusual—and perhaps auspicious—was the fact that the hospital had been completed during, and in spite of, routine Communist bombing on the Tai Chen islands nearby, and with the almost constant threat of invasion. There had been virtually no investment in foreign institutions, and Chinese faith in their own country had been at low ebb. Skepticism in the Chinese mind turned to confidence as they saw Americans building a substantial hospital near the nation's most prominent airfield. It was the only first-class hospital in Taipei, and almost from its opening day the Sanitarium was filled to its hallways with patients, most of whom were critically ill.

Madame Chiang seemed particularly pleased. "You see this beautiful hospital," she said with a gracious gesture toward its light gray façade. "It is now about to open for the people of Formosa. It cost a large amount of money, and probably all of you think that the Seventh-day Adventists are very rich people, that they build these hospitals all over the world. I happen to know that the Church is not made up of wealthy people. However, all of its people give a tenth of their income. If every person in the world would pay a tenth of his income for such things, what a blessing to humanity it would be."

Caring for both the Chinese and foreign patients in the crowded hospital was a strenuous day-and-night routine which began to tell on the aging surgeon. Early in 1956 Harry Miller asked to be relieved of his duties. "I was certainly delighted," he says, "when we received word that Dr. C. E. Randolph, another surgeon from China days, would come to share the burden with Dr. Brooks."

He and Mary made more honeymoon plans to travel, and then to settle down to their cherished nutritional research. They decided to make their exit as quickly and quietly as possible in order not to upset the community's confidence in the Sanitarium.

However, grateful friends would have no incognito departures. On the contrary, so many gifts, feasts, and parties were planned for the Millers that they were nearly killed with appreciation. First on the list were the women of the United States International Co-operation Administration. To Mary they presented a luxuriously embroidered housecoat, and to Harry a cash gift and a fine, engraved watch. More than forty of them who had been his patients also had their names engraved on a plaque which expressed to him their gratitude and veneration.

Meanwhile, secret plans for another event were being made. "One morning we were eating breakfast," Dr. Miller recalls, "when our houseboy walked in, held up his hand, and pushed out his thumb. This meant there was a big honor in store. He said that the Generalissimo was going to give me a fine present. But since the chap was sometimes a bit uncouth we paid little attention to him, thinking that he was just talking to make a good impression."

However, that forenoon when he made his rounds at the hospital the surgeon had to change bandages on one of his goiter patients, General Yang, whom he had treated at Hankow years before. As he entered Yang's room, the General propped himself up in his bed, extended his hand, and with a big smile said in Chinese:

"*Kongshi, Kongshi!* Congratulations!"

"Congratulations about what?" Miller asked.

"Oh, haven't you heard?" Yang acted surprised. "You are to receive the Government's highest honor."

Dr. Miller not only was unaware of such an event, but doubted that he deserved the honor were it to be offered. Later that day a courier delivered a large red envelope containing the Generalissimo's formal invitation for luncheon "on March 26 at the President's mansion." The doctor asked Miss Redelstein what she knew about it. She knew a great deal, but she was saying very little.

At the time appointed, Harry and Mary arrived at the mansion. They were ushered into a richly furnished room where a group of guests were waiting. Photographers appeared at every turn. The Millers had seldom known such treatment. A few moments after they were seated one of the staff cried out, "Madame Chiang Kai-shek," and everyone rose as the gracious lady made her entry, greeting each person by name and asking all to be seated. Next was announced, "Generalissimo Chiang Kai-shek," and everyone stood again.

The Generalissimo sat down with the Millers and began to ask about Taiwan Sanitarium. Did they have any particular needs he might fill? Harry dodged the question, expressing gratitude for what Chiang had done through the years, and taking care not to mention the occasion of the Generalissimo's last visit as a Miller patient—in Sian when he had injured his spine trying to escape from the Young Marshal. But there had been many earlier occasions, one of them being the time Miller had treated Chiang for a stomach disorder. The Generalissimo recalled that incident, and how he had become so fond of the Sanitarium's soy milk that he had sent his plane over a thousand miles from Kunming to Shanghai to replenish his supply. Being a health-minded couple, the Chiangs never thought it odd that the Millers were vegetarians, and they always served the Millers accordingly.

After the luncheon, the Generalissimo arose and made a brief speech, filled with many tidbits that Harry felt "were like a rich dessert, delicious in taste but embarrassing in quantity to a medical relic like me." With the statement that the Government had authorized him to present its highest decoration, the Generalissimo opened a little red case, took from it a beautiful gold medal, the coveted Blue Star of China, and pinned it on the missionary's chest. Then, taking a scroll from an aide, he unrolled it with great solemnity. It was inscribed by him, his foreign minister, and his minister of defense. The Generalissimo read it in Chinese and then asked his secretary to read a translation in English for the benefit of the foreign guests.

He next rolled it up and was about to hand it to Harry Miller, but before Chiang could extend his arm Madame Chiang took the scroll from him and handed it to Mary.

"Here, my dear," she said, "you also had a part in the building of our lovely hospital. A big part of the honor is yours!"

For months afterward, whether in Formosa, Hong Kong, the Philippines, or America, Harry and Mary Miller were met by the press. Harry Miller's two abiding concerns from the delightful occasion were that some of his friends in Communist China might not understand, and that others who had served with him through the years did not share in the honor. Before the ceremony Miss Redelstein had actually expressed fear to Madame Chiang that he might decline the medal. "Never mind," Madame had said, "there is no reason to fear. No one in the history of the Chinese Republic deserves it more than Dr. Miller."

It seemed to Harry and Mary Miller, when finally they were ready to leave Taipei, that all of their friends in China had come to the airport to see them off on their long-delayed honeymoon. It was one of those partings that is both sad and happy. The Chinese were indeed a part of Dr. Miller, but his weary frame looked forward to the rest which could not be found among them.

XXVII

BENGHAZI BRINK

IF THE MILLERS were looking forward to a quiet life of study and research, they would have to wait a while. A few weeks after they were settled in their new Arlington, California, home, the call from foreign fields again shattered their dreams. This time it was an emergency message from the Adventist hospital in the British island possession of Trinidad. Dr. David Bull, their surgeon, had to have rest, and Dr. R. F. Dunlop could not handle alone the two hundred patients daily crowding clinics and surgery schedules. Miller did have a British license, it was pointed out.

Harry and Mary found the Indians and Negroes of Trinidad an interesting change from the peoples of China. Miller and Dunlop worked four examining tables apiece, screening out the less needy, hospitalizing the seriously ill, but prescribing treatment for all.

Dr. Miller reports: "As in other hospitals a large number of our patients were pregnant women. But we were surprised to find that many of them in Trinidad frankly registered themselves as unmarried mothers. It was not a matter of immorality to them, but of necessity. There apparently was a shortage of eligible men, but that did not matter. They wanted to be mothers, wedlock or no. And mothers they became."

It was in 1956, at Libya, that Dr. Miller found himself involved in one of the most moving events of his long life. By then Harry

Miller had overrun by seven years his allotted threescore and ten. Seventy-seven certainly seemed a reasonable age at which to wish to depart the nerve-tensioned environs of the operating room for a quieter life at Arlington and Mount Vernon. Also, Mary wanted to take a few months to finish her music degree at the University of Cincinnati. She was willing and anxious to rest awhile after the post-to-post flights of the past three years.

Then, as if with split-second timing by Fate's experienced hand, all their dreams were blown from the California foothills to Africa's desert sands. Late the same night that Mary presented her graduation recital, she received by telephone word of her father's death. Dr. Miller had already left for Chicago an hour before on a long-scheduled business trip. Returning immediately to Cincinnati for the funeral, he received an urgent telephone call. It was from Washington, D.C., asking him to go post haste to Libya for two months.

"Dr. Roy Cornell, the medical director of our hospital at Benghazi, has been stricken with bulbar polio," reported Dr. Ted Flaiz, the General Conference medical secretary. "He is totally paralyzed and in critical condition."

"What is the prognosis?" Harry Miller asked.

"Little hope that he'll survive," Flaiz replied.

"How much time do we have?" was Miller's next query.

"Cornell is the only physician there, and the hospital is full. You can judge for yourself," came the answer.

Dr. Miller recalls: "Momentarily, I had no idea where Libya was, not to mention Benghazi. I faintly recollected reading about it in connection with the battles of the Second World War between the desert armies of Rommel and Wavell. But I had a better idea of what it meant to Roy Cornell to be struck down helplessly by disease while trying to pioneer a hospital in that isolated North African city. The specific need was for an experienced surgeon with a British medical license. I knew we must go."

He promised to call Dr. Flaiz right after the funeral. Even before the casket was lowered, Miller's mind was moving toward

North Africa. The next day the Millers sent to Washington for necessary visas, and a few days later they were en route by Air France from New York to Tripoli, by way of Paris, Rome, and Malta.

At Tripoli, Libya's capital city, they had to wait overnight for their Benghazi flight. Despite Tripoli's favored Mediterranean location on Africa's northwestern coast, the heat was oppressive. The hectic trip, together with the high temperature, wilted them beyond belief. They arose early in the morning and headed for the beach, hoping for respite. But there was none.

Eleven o'clock found the Millers at the airport, ready for departure. They were soon escorted to the little plane. The desert sun was high in the sky, and the airport thermometer registered one hundred seventeen degrees in the shade. After waiting in the frying pan of a cabin while the pilot warmed up the engine, they "almost decided to walk." As if reading their minds, the airline officials called them back to the terminal. The weather was too hot to fly, the officials said. So Harry and Mary sat under the waiting-room fans for another four hours until the weather cooled off a bit and they could wing on to Benghazi.

At the Benghazi airfield the Millers were met by the hospital group with the same unabashed joy of fellowship they had found typical of missionary meetings everywhere. Dr. William Wagner was there from Iraq's Baghdad Adventist Hospital, having flown to Benghazi to keep things going until the Millers arrived.

Dr. Cornell was in the British military hospital, where he was being cared for as skillfully as the difficult circumstances permitted. The British had performed a tracheotomy, running a small tube through the front of his neck down into his windpipe. To this was connected a little machine which forced air in and out to provide respiration. They further managed to keep him alive by frequent bathing, turning, and careful rubbing. This continued until a memorable Fourth of July when the American Air Force moved in with an iron lung and specialists to evacuate Cornell to Seattle, where he began a tedious fight to regain muscular control. It is a battle that he is still waging today.

Meanwhile, the picture at Benghazi was not encouraging. In his year of pioneering the hospital, Dr. Cornell had become greatly beloved by the community, and few people there were willing to settle for anyone else. It was the only mission-operated hospital in Libya, and it was generally regarded as the best civilian medical institution in Benghazi. Roy Cornell had built up enviable obstetrical and surgical departments in addition to operating an excellent general medicine program. At thirty-eight, he was young, enthusiastic, medically progressive, and doing well in the Arabic language.

In his place came Dr. Miller, apparently an aging, white-haired relic from China. Furthermore, and unfortunately, Chinese and Arabic are not sister tongues. At Benghazi, Miller had to work through an interpreter, and he says: "I have yet to find an interpreter who really gets the doctor's personality across." Perhaps reflecting his own fears a pall of despair seemed to come over the people of that city. Certainly the already overworked hospital staff were disheartened and depressed. Then, as a final blow, the nurse in charge of the X-ray department became ill and was forced to return to Cairo.

Within two weeks of his arrival, Harry Miller was brought face to face with a situation that seemed to be like the last block on the little boy's stack—the one that knocks them all down. Roy Cornell had become a good friend of Dr. D. Moawad, chief of Libya's medical service, and Moawad frequently sent patients to Cornell. That fine, friendly doctor brought Miller the last patient in the world he wanted to see—an aged lady in diabetic coma.

"I am dreadfully sorry to bring you this patient," Dr. Moawad apologized.

"I am not sure what we can do," Miller told him less than enthusiastically.

"You see I am a surgeon," the Libyan continued, "and I really know little about medical cases such as this. Besides, she comes from a very important family."

"Oh!" the American exclaimed under his breath. "Do you have any more bad news?"

He reached for the wrist of the patient. She was wet with a cold sweat, which told him she was in shock. Almost without pulse, she breathed as if each breath were her last. Miller's few days in Libya had been long enough for him to learn that the superstitious natives do not hesitate to blame the doctor for a death. Her death could be the fatal blow to the hospital project.

The patient was, in fact, a relative of the king. Her two sons were prominent bankers. To multiply complexity, a group of high-ranking officials was gathering at the bedside.

Miller knew he must get some fluids into her bloodstream immediately to antagonize her high blood sugar. But, alas, he found her veins collapsed. No matter how feverishly he worked, he could not get a needle into the vessels. Finally he left the room. Stepping out with him, Dr. Moawad spoke half in a whisper:

"Doctor, if I were you I wouldn't try anything else, because if she dies they might blame you for hastening her death!"

Moawad did not need to tell him twice!

"What do you suggest?" the American asked.

"Nothing," was his reply. "She is going to die anyway!"

Under the circumstances this made sense. Humanly speaking, they were plainly on the brink of disaster. Even at best the remains of the dwindling reputation of the hospital were on the block. All the surgeon could do was to keep on praying, as he had from the moment the woman had been brought in.

At that point Miriam Bruce, a keen-minded and influential American nurse, moved over to the patient's sons, who were waiting at their mother's side.

"Why don't you ask Dr. Miller to go ahead? If he felt a little freer he might be able to bring your mother through."

"Yes, yes!" they pleaded. "Have him try anything, anything."

"And you will not hold him responsible if she dies?"

"No, no. It's all on us. It's all on us," they kept reiterating. "Just do anything you can."

With that encouragement, Miller placed a blood-pressure cuff around the patient's arm. It allowed the blood from the arteries to flow out, but prevented that in the veins from returning. This puffed out the collapsed veins sufficiently to enable him to insert the needle for intravenous medication. Then he began a night-long vigil, to the great surprise and admiration of the relatives, who did not expect a foreign surgeon to extend himself very much for a Libyan patient. What they did not know was that the harried surgeon had anxieties from another quarter. During the stress of those first few weeks his Mary had also burned both ends of her bright candle. Cooking and caring for the influx of visitors during their early days, and using strange foods under unfamiliar circumstances, had told on the normally vigorous young woman. Now she was critically ill with infectious hepatitis. Jaundiced and fevered, she responded slowly in the strange African weather. Dr. Miller nursed her day and night between his surgery, clinic, and hospital schedules. Perhaps because he had lost Maude and Marie, he was all the more determined not to lose Mary. Her will to live brought a happy response to his care.

But, for his Libyan patient, except for the fact that she was still alive, there was little in her condition to encourage the doctor. The elderly lady continued unconscious through the second day and night, and Dr. Miller remained at her side every possible moment. The third day, although still in coma, she showed improvement in circulation and pulse, and the weary surgeon finally went to bed. On the fourth morning, Miller walked into the room to find the patient's sons beaming through their tears.

"Mother recognized us," they said fervently. And there she was, propped up in bed, eyes open, smiling.

A few minutes later Dr. Moawad came in to make his daily visit. When he saw the patient, he grabbed Harry Miller's arm in sheer exuberation.

"Dr. Miller," he exclaimed to the delight of all, "a miracle has happened!"

The news of her recovery spread like fire in stubble. The fact of Dr. Miller's abiding care was not lost. "A dying woman has been cured by the devoted American doctor," was the word that flashed from sector to sector and house to house. It was picked up by the embassies and the American and British communities. Before long, the hospital was filled, and the daily clinics were so crowded that the staff could hardly handle them. As with Benny the hunchback in Washington, D.C., and as with countless crises in China, it was apparent to Harry Miller that God, in His infinite wisdom, had used an impossible situation to turn the tide.

At first the Millers had no idea that Libya would be such a bright spot in their lives. "We had our share of rough times," says Harry Miller, "and the two months lengthened to five. We did not see much of Libya but we saw plenty of Libya's sick. We had as many as sixty clinic patients each forenoon in addition to our hospital cases, our surgery schedules, and of course the ever-flowing stream of babies. When Dr. J. P. Munsey came to take the helm, we were glad to release it to younger, more energetic hands."

One of the most satisfying experiences in later life is the recognition of Divine leading in the choice of one's career. Such influences may not be too easily understood in the earlier years of living; but, as time passes, and growth makes a person more sensitive to appreciate forces and even small causes that have shaped his course of life, he becomes aware of circumstances that have guided him. With thoughts of such circumstances filling his mind, Harry Miller, white-haired and slightly stooped, celebrated his eightieth birthday on July 1, 1959. At that time, Art Linkletter and other radio and television stars joined the press in covering the surgeon-scientist's "retirement." But indications are that retirement is not yet at hand. Recently, Clarence Miller left his brother a substantial bequest. "Uncle Sam and the lawyers took most of it," the doctor says, "but we have a job to do with the rest."

The job? He went again to the Orient at eighty-one, to start a new hospital in Hong Kong as well as an exciting new chapter in world nutrition. In Japan, the alert Ministry of Health has invited missionary Miller to take the lead in the establishment of small soy-milk plants in each one of the thirty thousand village tofu factories of that nation.

While the social scientists worry about the population explosion, Harry Miller is taking practical steps to feed the famished through new uses for long-known foods. From Japan, he sees his gospel of nourishment fanning out over the world. And in its wake, he believes, the good news of Christ will follow more readily, for empty stomachs are not a preacher's soil. Healed minds and happy hearts depend on healthy, nourished bodies. In order to perpetuate the work he has begun, Dr. Miller has placed its future direction in the hands of the Harry W. Miller Foundation of New York City, whose officers share his determination to achieve medical progress and nutritional advance throughout the world.

There is a secret which must be learned before the sun will shine again over China and the world, before the chains of weariness and oblivion will be loosed, before the shackles of blight and starvation are broken. The secret does not reside in the crimson flag of the Communist, nor wholly in technology's rewards. Rather, it lies largely in the hearts of men who have learned in the refining furnace of selfless service to love their neighbors as themselves. They are the ones who know the Author of love and who are able to convey the heartfelt assurance of His grace.

On the day the giant jet liner again carried Harry Miller away from his homeland and back to the Orient he loves, those who saw him off felt sure that the China Doctor is such a man. He has known the agonies of disease and desperation, and the threat of death. And, following his God, he has gone many times and willingly into a darkling night to help bring the light of eternal day.

INDEX

211